# Get Your Sparkle Back

*How to re-ignite your health, happiness, energy and confidence.*

## SALLY BEATON

This book's for any woman who's lost her sparkle…

**British Library Cataloguing in Publication Data**

A catalogue record for this book is available from the British Library.

ISBN 978-1-9161302-0-3 (pbk)
ISBN 978-1-9161302-1-0 (ebk)

*Publisher: Sparkle Books Publishing*
*Cover photography and artwork: ollieweaitphotography.com*
*Original cover design: dariabalashova.com*

*"This book is going to change lives…"*
*Ariane Signer*


*"An absolute staple for every woman's bookshelf…*
*I only wish I had read this years ago…"*
*Helen Hanson*


*"What a book! "*
*Carly Moosah*


*"This is so important…"*
*Charlie Baker*

# Contents

"For a star to be born, there is one thing that must happen: a gaseous nebula must collapse.
So collapse.
Crumble.
This is not your destruction.
This is your birth."

*Author Nikka Ursula*
*(@nikkaursula)*

# FOREWORD

by Carly Moosah

A wise woman once said to me, "I sense you pour so much of yourself into everyone else that there's little left for you." She was right. She told me it was time for me to start caring for and investing in myself. That wise woman, who has changed my life with her knowledge, wisdom, and relentless championing of women, has now written this book. I know her knowledge, love, and wisdom can change your life, too.

Sally is always teaching, coaching, and encouraging women to be nothing less than the best version of themselves. This book is a goddesses' manual that will teach you how to do just that. I believe this book will give you many of the answers you've been desperately seeking as a woman and enable you to once more be your most fabulous, sparkly self. Sally is a cheerleader of women like no other. Without question, by the time you put this book down, it will have you cheerleading and loving yourself.

*Get Your Sparkle Back* is essential for every woman's bookshelf because I know it can do for you what it did for me – which was open my eyes to what love and respect for myself feels like after a lifetime of living without either. My life has changed for the better from hearing and reading Sally's words, and now I'm so excited that so many other women will have access to this magic to improve their lives and get their sparkle back, too.

# INTRODUCTION

I don't know how you came to find this book or why you've lost a little or lot of your sparkle. I don't know if your sparkle was taken from you or, if little by little you gave it away. Whatever the reason, I'm so glad you're here.

If you feel like your energy, confidence, and passion for life have all taken a nose-dive, I hear you. If you feel like you've lost yourself and your sparkle, I get it. I've been there (more than once) and it's no fun. But, let me tell you from personal experience – you *can* get your sparkle back.

You see, despite what you think or have been told, your sparkle wasn't destined to decline with age. It wasn't meant to be obliterated by tragedy, childbirth, or trying times. Feeling anxious, depressed, insecure, stressed, ill, totally exhausted, or unhappy with your body all of the time just isn't the life you were created for. You were created to sparkle.

Your sparkle is as unique as your fingerprint and can often be difficult to describe or define. A woman with her sparkle may have a vibrant energy, spring in her step, and glint in her eye. She may be someone comfortable in her own skin who isn't concerned with competing with other women. She may live her life loudly and relentlessly pursue her passions or, she may possess a quiet, peaceful, contentment and confidence that you're drawn to. A woman with sparkle may have a 'joie de vivre' that's evident for all to see or perhaps she sparkles silently just for herself. A woman with sparkle may be the life

7

and soul of the party or a woman who prefers to be alone and nap when her body asks her to. A woman may not even know that she's living with her sparkle, but she'll undoubtedly know when she isn't.

It doesn't matter if you can't quite pinpoint the elements that create your sparkle or are currently missing from your life – perhaps it's energy, fun, self-confidence, sexiness, all of the above or something else – you just have to know you can get it back.

Getting your sparkle back isn't a cute concept to momentarily boost you and I don't want you thinking it's all about wearing sequins and dancing round disco balls (although personally I hope it involves both those things). Getting your sparkle back is about you being able to experience your happiest, healthiest life again. A life that feels exciting, not exhausting. A life that's not about people pleasing and 'putting up' with stuff, but one that has purpose and passion. A life you feel you're truly living and not merely existing in.

Me? Well, I'm a women's holistic nutritionist and life coach, aka a 'Sparkle Coach', and I've helped women of all ages, all over the world to get their sparkle back. The reason I believe I'm so good at this is because I've been through tough challenges – both mentally and physically – that snuffed my sparkle out. I then spent years learning about the things that can help boost or reduce a woman's sparkle as I made my way back to my own. I believe I have some of the best strategies that can help women struggling with their sparkle. And now, something previously only reserved for my 1-2-1 clients, I'm going to share them with you.

In these sparkly pages, you're going to learn how to understand your hormones so you can start to feel mentally and physically fabulous again; how to boost your energy so you don't feel tired *all* the time; how it's possible to pursue the dreams you have in your heart (but may be too embarrassed to say out loud); how you can feel confident with how you look, who you are and get back to being the most sparkly version of yourself again. Sound good?

The secret to making my sparkle formulas work for you though, is to take the information in this book and adapt it to your own life, goals, and circumstances. There should never be a prescriptive "one size fits all" approach from any book, coach, diet plan, person, or program that you follow, so please keep this in mind as we journey together.

Right then, you ready? Let's go get your sparkle back…

# SCIENCE OF YOUR
# SPARKLE

Throughout this book, I'm going to delve into different ways that I believe can help you get your sparkle back. I want us to start by creating a firm sparkle-filled foundation so you can start building a body and life that's balanced, bursting with health, and sparkles at its very core. I want you to feel like the best, most energised, centred, and confident version of yourself, and to understand if you don't feel like this, then why? I'd love you to learn from one of the biggest sparkle-stealing times of my life in the hope you never have to go through the same mental and physical pain that I did, simply because I (or the professionals around me) didn't understand the science and cycle of my female body.

Every woman should be taught what I'm going to teach you in this chapter. I believe it's eye-opening, exciting, and a fundamental part of getting your sparkle back. I'm going to give you the basic instruction manual for how your incredible female body works cyclically each month. If you're currently having periods then this is essential reading for you. However, if for whatever reason you're not, there's also important and uplifting information for you in this chapter too. After over a decade of believing my mental health was a mess and my physical health a mystery, this knowledge has freed me. I now see my body and mind as a source of strength, stability, and sparkle instead of being crazy, chaotic, and unpredictable – and I want the same for you.

So, how are you feeling? Do you feel healthy and vibrant? Do you feel a bit 'blah'? Are you constantly battling different physical and/or emotional symptoms? Do you enjoy being around people one day, then the next feel exhausted and want to be left alone? Well, don't worry! It's very normal, but not at all necessary to feel confused and frustrated by the constant shifts your mind and body goes through. I'm going to help you unlock a new way of living that shows you're not an unpredictable, irrational woman at the mercy of her hormones but actually, you're a naturally cyclical being with a reliable health and sparkle-boosting rhythm. It's time for you to step off that rollercoaster you've been riding with constant ups and downs in your energy, appetite, weight, and mood because living that way steals your health, happiness, and sparkle.

Let me quickly tell you a little of my own journey so you can understand how I was able to move from struggling to getting my sparkly self back…

## Ignoring The Signs

Growing up, I'd been an effortlessly sparkly child. I was naturally optimistic and upbeat. Bar a few moody teenage years, this outlook on life continued till my mid-20's when I began to struggle both mentally and physically. I experienced adult acne, mood swings, cripplingly painful periods, unexplained weight gain, exhaustion, and was diagnosed with Irritiable Bowel Syndrome (IBS) and Polycystic Ovary Syndrome (PCOS) – as you can see, I was quite the catch. I just seemed to go from one horrible symptom and diagnoses to the next.

These health problems carried on for nearly a decade with no real help or resolution – just a constant variety of pills prescribed to "try" and see if they'd help and a shoulder shrug coupled with a, "Well, this is just what happens to some women." Then, when I was thirty, I was diagnosed with a cystosarcoma phyllodes (a rare, fast-growing breast tumour) and had to have two operations to remove it.

I believed I had a fragile, unstable mind, and a crappy, unreliable body that kept getting sick and that this was just how life was for me now. I believed I was some sort of ticking time bomb and was sure I'd develop another tumour – only this time I panicked I'd not be so lucky and find it in time (with the words of my consultant echoing in my ears "If this had been discovered 6 months later, we'd be in all sorts of trouble"). I thought all the conditions I'd struggled with for years and years were all unrelated – because that's how they were treated by my doctors – and merely confirmed I had a defective body that kept going wrong in various places.

Four months after my second operation, as people tried to kindly encourage me that it was time to "get back to normal", I sat crying in another shapeless nightie to disguise the body I no longer felt safe in. I missed the old me so much – the happy, carefree, lover of life that ten years previously believed anything was possible for her life. A woman whose body was just there to help her have fun, work hard, and reach her dreams. I desperately wanted to get her back because I couldn't believe that this depressed, scared (and now also scarred) person was who I was saddled with for the rest of my life. I remember thinking, "Oh, so this is why lots of women become more miserable as they get older – life overwhelms them, sad stuff happens, they get sick, and without any warning their sparkle goes." I hated that this sad, sparkle-less state was now my present and seemed to be my future.

As the months went by and I was trying to learn how to exist as the new fragile and fearful version of me, I began to feel thoroughly fed up with being a patient, victim, and someone people smiled sadly at as they asked, "How are you doing?" I didn't want to just accept that I was now a sad, sparkle-less woman who's conversations centred around illnesses and how unfair life felt – that just didn't feel like the *real* me. That didn't feel like the life I, or any woman, was created to have.

I knew if I saw my friend, who was once previously full of life and fun, have her sparkle suffocated, I'd try to help her out. I'd do whatever it took. So, I decided to try and do the same for myself, even though I had minimal energy or inclination. However, there was still a flicker of sparkle inside of me that was encouraging me to not let the feelings of darkness totally consume me. To not permanently become someone I knew at my core I wasn't. I wanted to laugh, have fun, be silly, be sexy, plan adventures, live my life to the full and achieve my dreams. Not just miserably wait for my next scan or doctor's appointment to tell me I was still tumour free or that there was a new medication to try.

I decided it was time to become my own health detective and trace my steps back to when I did have my health and sparkle. The questions I wanted answered for starters were: Why had I experienced so many different physical problems throughout my 20's? Why did I feel so depressed? What was the root cause of me getting a rare breast tumour at 30? The doctors couldn't answer my questions with anything more than generalisations like, "We don't know," and, "These things just happen to some women" which were no longer good enough answers for me.

So, I did my own digging into my health. I mapped out all of my health problems from the previous decade and what I discovered was jaw-dropping. I found out that despite what I'd believed, I didn't have a defective body with numerous unconnected issues and problems. I'd only ever had ONE problem – I had imbalanced hormones! After years of being prescribed a variety of pills for my variety of ills, no doctor had ever looked at me as a whole person (hence why I now practice holistic nutrition) and realised that I was a woman so mentally and physically stressed that my body was chronically inflamed. This inflammation was stopping my hormones from being happy, healthy, and working in harmony.

The biggest problem seemed to be that I had way too much oestrogen (known as 'oestrogen dominance') and this was one of the main causes of my acne, mood swings, painful and heavy periods, weight gain, exhaustion, IBS, PCOS, breast tumour, and other issues. For over a decade, my body had tried to wave little 'white flags' with these various symptoms to tell me something was wrong with how I was living. That I was out of balance and that it needed me to help it, not ignore it or suppress the symptoms it was giving me with another pill.

My body had tried to show me that it was struggling to cope with the huge amounts of physical and emotional stressors and toxins in my life, and was being prevented from doing its job properly of keeping me in vibrant, sparkly health. The first sign it gave me of "Hey Sal, the way you're living life right now isn't great for us," was the confidence-shattering adult acne which some days was so inflamed with cystic boils on my jawline that it hurt to open my mouth or smile. I would have to sit with ice packs and think of excuses to not have to see people because I was so embarrassed of my appearance.

I tried to suppress this symptom with various pills and harsh lotions, all of which were offered to me as potential cures for this 'external' condition. Spoiler alert: it was actually an internal problem showing up externally due to my diet containing lots of inflammatory dairy, alcohol, and sugar and a lifestyle containing lots of emotional stress and weight loss attempts. I now know *that's* what was causing my hormonal acne, not that my skin was in need of strong medications or harsh topical creams.

Next, I experienced PMS so overwhelming and periods so heavy and painful I'd be doubled over in pain, feeling like I was going to either faint or vomit, and I often had to miss days of work when this happened. Did I take notice of these cries of help from my body, asking to be listened to and given some extra love and attention? Nope. I simply asked my doctors what pill I needed to try next to stop the pain because I'd been brought up in a society that believed your health was either good or not, and if it wasn't good then it was a doctor who needed to make it better with a pill. It's only now I've learnt that these pills (which can of course be needed and helpful short-term) often just mask the symptoms, not heal your body in the long-term.

I really had no idea that my health is almost entirely down to the decisions I make on a daily, even hourly basis. The doctors were essentially playing 'whack-a-mole' with my various health conditions and never looking at the root cause of why my body was feeling so crappy. This meant when one symptom had been silenced by a medication, another would 'pop-up' and the severity seemed to increase each time. After various scans and hospital appointments for my pain and problem periods, I was given the diagnoses (or what felt like a horrible badge to wear) of PCOS and IBS. When I asked about long-term solutions, more shoulder shrugs and medications followed, along with being unsympathetically told things like I'd likely struggle to have children and could grow a beard. I mean, come on people, talk about knowing how to kick a girl when she's down.

Despite all of these symptoms raging, all I wanted to do was ignore them, medicate over them, and carry on working and partying hard. I saw my body like jockeys see racehorses – something to be whipped, pushed to the limits, and exerted no matter the long-term cost or consequences. I wasn't listening to my body and so it was escalating my symptoms to try and get my attention – it was like someone having to shout increasingly loudly to the person next to them who has their fingers in their ears and is singing, "la, la, la, I'm not listening."

I didn't think I needed to listen to my body because that's what I trusted the doctors to do. I saw them as demi-gods and believed that if there was a reason for all I was going through or a cure then they'd surely know about it. I didn't realise they were simply looking at individual symptoms as if I was a car with a few faulty bits that quickly needed fixing. When what I actually needed them to do was heed the 'warning lights' of my body in the symptoms it was producing. I needed my doctors to look at me as a whole interconnected woman and try to figure out the best long-term healing path for the desperate and depressed woman before them, not just switch off the warning lights so I could continue my unhealthy and dangerous lifestyle. I'm not saying I should never have been prescribed pills to try and get me out of my pain – this was often a great relief and very needed, but it should have gone hand in hand with trying to figure out the root cause issues in my body.

I'm not bashing all doctors. There are some total angels out there, some of whom I've had the pleasure of being helped by, but they work within a healthcare system that all too often belittles "womens problems" and tries to get rid of our symptoms. This is like constantly putting sticky tape over a child's mouth to stop them screaming and just using stronger and stronger tape if the first didn't work. The most sensible, good, kind, and loving idea would be to find out the reason the child is screaming.

Another analogy is that when you get a health symptom – be it mental or physical – it's like having a leak in your ceiling. You can of course decide to "fix" the problem by covering the leak with a patch on the ceiling and a bucket below to catch any drips. But if you don't take time to find out why and where the water's coming from into your house, it can be super dangerous. If the leak carries on with no further, deeper investigation then your whole ceiling could collapse and cause untold damage.

For years I ignored the 'leaks' coming from my body that were signaling my body's chronic inflammation and hormonal imbalance. So, eventually the 'roof' of my health did fall in when I got my breast tumour diagnosis and had to go through the subsequent operations to remove it. I actually felt like my whole world had collapsed at that time. But, after decades of ignoring my body and suppressing its symptoms, *finally* it had my attention. I was now ready to listen to the reason it had been screaming at me through my acne, heavy periods, IBS, and PCOS. I was ready to find out the source and cause of the 'leaks' and not just patch up my body with another pill only for another 'leak' to spring up somewhere else.

I was ready to take my fingers out of my ears and start a two-way conversation with my body because I wanted my health, life, and sparkle back. I wanted to take back my personal power and not leave my health in the hands of doctors like I'd been doing for years. I wanted to do all I could, every single day, to reduce the chronic inflammation in my body so I could balance my hormones, get rid of my horrible symptoms, and bring balance and health back to my body. My health was now *my* responsibility and I was no longer going to outsource it to anyone else. For the first time in a long time I felt empowered not exhausted by this idea.

**It's Down To Me**

Did you know that the majority of chronic health conditions including heart disease, cancer, diabetes, and Alzheimer's (in fact over 90-95%) are not genetic predispositions that we have no control over? In fact, most health problems arise from a cause and effect situation. That is, they are caused by what we eat, drink, think, what's in our environment, and how we live our lives. It's *not* from bad luck or because it's just something that's "in the family", which is what I'd been led to believe.

My unhappy health situations hadn't come out of the blue like I thought, and my breast tumour hadn't sprung up overnight (in fact most tumours take about 8-10 years to grow and become detectable in the body). I started to realise how I'd been living for the past decade was much more likely the cause of all the health problems I'd experienced as opposed to my belief I had a defective body. Since my early 20's, I'd been trying to force a career in the music industry; racked up debts trying to keep up with a lifestyle I couldn't afford; was worried about my parents who were struggling with health issues; was a long-term people pleaser who wanted to keep all of my friends, colleagues and partners happy (btw, this isn't possible) and stayed in a variety of stressful, toxic relationships far longer than I should've.

Added to these things, I never rested. I was constantly trying to impress people and prove my worth in the world because I didn't feel good enough as I was. I was using hormone-disrupting beauty products and chemical-laden cleaning products on a daily basis. I yo-yo dieted, ate crappy food, and drank *a lot* of alcohol. I had zero knowledge of my female body and how the health of my menstrual cycle was linked to my overall mental and physical health.

My body couldn't cope with all of these stressors and that resulted in chronic inflammation. This threw my hormones out of whack resulting in me having excessively high levels oestrogen, which was one of the biggest causes of my painful heavy periods, PCOS, IBS, low moods, weight gain and then eventually a breast tumour*.

Luckily, my own health detective work found the source of my 'leak'. This meant that I could look to reduce my inflammation, bring my hormones back into balance, and not carry on with the sparkle-suppressing health problems of the previous decade.

I'm going to give you a variety of ways throughout this book to help you reduce inflammation in your body so you can help bring your hormones and body back into balance. But, first I want to tell you about a certain group of your hormones and how they powerfully affect your daily life. I want you to know that even understanding this can help reduce your stress and some of the negative mental and physical symptoms you may be experiencing throughout your month. Learning about the monthly ebb and flow of the hormones linked with your menstrual cycle** is a huge factor in you being able to get your sparkle back. It has the power to boost your mental and physical health as you begin to understand your moods, appetite, energy, and overall wellbeing – possibly for the first time in your life.

*It's important to say, if you have symptoms like acne, PMS, heavy or painful periods, have been diagnosed with IBS, or PCOS , please don't get yourself in a panic. It doesn't mean you'll get a breast tumour like I did. It does however mean your body is trying to get your attention through these symptoms, and I suggest you could be suffering from chronic inflammation and a hormonal imbalance. The sparkly tips in this book may be enough to help eliminate your symptoms. However, if not, then I'd encourage you to look at your whole life and body and not just the part that's in pain. Book in with a holistic practitioner like a functional medicine doctor, naturopath, holistic nutritionist, or homeopath *(basically anyone who'll look at your body as a whole), so they can help you get to the root cause of your health problems and bring your beautiful body back into balance. If this isn't something you can currently afford then the reading list at the back of this book will be a great place for you to start becoming your own health detective and finding answers.*

*\*\*If you're not currently having periods for any reason, have had a hysterectomy, or gone through a natural or chemical menopause, please keep reading! There's important info included for you, too.*

## Your AMAZING Female Body – Cyclical Not Unpredictable

A crucial part of me feeling empowered and seeing my body as an ally, not an enemy ready to stab me in the back with a new symptom or illnesses at any point, was understanding my female hormones and the phases of my menstrual cycle. This knowledge was utterly life-changing for me (and is for my clients, too). I believe learning this is the key to women feeling in control of their mental and physical health in their fertile years and beyond. There's not one woman I've taught this to who hasn't been blown away by it and also a little bit angry (and rightly so) she wasn't taught it in school.

If you're having periods, you probably know that you go through a 28-day (or thereabouts) cycle. That's perhaps where your knowledge ends, though. You probably think, like I did till the age of thirty-five, that you only have two phases each month: 1) Having your period – which is horrible, draining, painful, and all together crappy and 2) Not having your period – which is generally a bit less crappy and lets you live a more "normal" life.

Here's the thing – you actually have 4 distinct hormonal phases in your menstrual cycle, that each have a huge emotional and physical impact on you. They affect your energy, appetite, mood, desire to be around people or not, ability to focus on certain tasks, your libido, and so much more. Not knowing about these phases and when the shifts occur can impact your relationships and health and leave you feeling confused and overwhelmed. Working with these hormonal phases can help re-empower and reinvigorate you. You'll realise there's regularity not randomness to your mental and physical shifts. You'll feel more in control of seemingly uncontrollable things (like your mood, energy, and appetite) and know how to feel healthy, happy, centred, and full of sparkle any time of your month, even on your period – I kid you not!

Your monthly female hormonal cycle is a health-boosting blessing (stick with me on this one, I promise to validate this audacious claim). It's not a messy mistake or curse like so many of us feel or have been taught. Each month, just like the moon (which has roughly the same length cycle as a woman) you go through 4 hormonal phases that mirror the changing seasons of the Earth. The problem is you've been taught to ignore the changing seasons of the Earth. I'm guessing you work and sleep roughly the same hours in winter as you do in summer. Do you have any idea what phase the moon's in or what phase of your own cycle you're in? I'm not shaming you, I'm just showing you we live in a world with powerful seasons that we ignore. More so, we live in bodies with powerful seasons that we also normally ignore.

You've been taught these things don't matter or have an effect on your normal day to day life. But, women were never meant to be this disconnected from their natural environment or rhythm of their own bodies. This disconnection or suppression is causing serious physical and mental side effects in many women. Why? Because most women have unknowingly been forced to live like men in a world set up by and for men. This has been one of the biggest things to damage many women's health.

Let me explain... **This Is A Man's World!**

Men have a hormonal cycle as well, but theirs is a 24-hour one. Yep, next time a man gets cranky because he's hungry or tired at a certain point in the day, you can tell him to "stop being so hormonal" or ask him if it's his "time of the day". Men's testosterone (if their hormones are balanced) starts off high in the morning, meaning they generally have extra focus, energy, and alertness first thing and this then decreases throughout the day. This is why there's so much focus and noise about sticking to a morning routine for ultimate success in life.

Early morning exercise boot-camps, gym sessions, business breakfast meetings, and even journaling are now the norm and championed as the things we should all be doing every day to be successful and healthy humans. Any deviation from this formula is seen as a lack of motivation, willpower, or desire for success. It's not – it's just easier for men to do this routine because they're generally hard-wired to feel and do the same things at the same time *every single day*. In the same way women are generally hard-wired to feel and do the same things at the same time *every single month*. However, it's the male 24-hour cycle that the world's been largely set up to run by and accommodate.

Many women around the world have been forced for centuries to live in this hectic, unrelenting, linear, masculine, 24-hour world where the focus is on constant productivity and growth. This doesn't fit in with our bodies and make-up which is a cyclical, seasonal, feminine, 28-day (or there abouts) pattern. This unrelenting masculine schedule goes against women's natural rhythm of life and is causing an abundance of illness and overwhelm. It's likely one of the reasons so many women are feeling depressed, despondent, and disconnected from their body, lives, and sparkle. They feel unable to cope with the constant daily demands put on them. Women being forced to live by the hormonal pattern of men has increased self-criticism, burnout, and the negative emotional and physical symptoms experienced by far too many women during their menstrual cycles. This is something I sadly see all the time in my online clinic.

For a woman to constantly have to live by the male 24-hour hormonal cycle instead of her own hormonal cycle is like a farmer planting seeds every day and trying to grow every type of vegetable all the time. This wouldn't work. The farmer has to use the crucial knowledge of whether it's the right season to plant and grow something or not. So if you feel like your life isn't blooming, flourishing or producing the things you want it to, it's time to start working with your fabulous female calendar so you can begin to grow the things in your life you want to.

It's one of the most natural, productive, beautiful, and nourishing rhythms there is for your life as a woman. Life suddenly becomes easier when you live how you're meant to, not how you've been told to. Your monthly cycle has been created so you can thrive as a woman and live a healthy, happy, and sparkle-filled life instead of regularly feeling exhausted, overwhelmed, anxious, unbalanced, or upset. So, let's get into the nitty gritty of your different hormonal phases so you can find out how to start living a sparkle, not stress, filled life.

## The Four Seasons

Let me take you on a tour of the 4 distinct phases or 'seasons' that your female hormones go through each month. Once you get to know these shifts you can begin to live the way you were meant to, not the way you've been told. You'll reap the health and sparkle-boosting benefits of understanding what your mind and body are doing (or should be doing if your hormones are balanced):

### Follicular Phase

*This is the start of a new cycle. It begins when the bleeding from your period ends.*

*Lasts approximately 7-10 days.*

**The sparkly season:**

This phase of your monthly cycle can be likened to Spring. It's when you're emerging from Winter (your period) and starting to see signs of 'new life' with physical and mental energy appearing again. This phase is what's known as an 'outward facing' season, which means you'll likely be drawn to being around people and being 'out and about' in the world.

**The sparkly science:**

Your follicle-stimulating hormone (FSH) and luteinising hormone (LH) levels are increasing to help your eggs mature. It's the beginning of the process of your uterine lining rebuilding itself after your period. Your oestrogen is increasing.

**What does this *actually* mean?**

**Mood**

It means you've got high levels of hormones that are designed to trigger the process of a potential new life. So, in this phase, your brain and body are wired to want to start and try new things.

If you don't, you'll likely feel frustrated, annoyed, and like your life is pretty dull and boring. Ever wondered why one week you're happy sitting on the sofa every night watching TV, and then the next you feel like your life and relationships are super boring? Chances are it was your follicular phase making your body and mind feel this way.

So, this is the phase of your monthly cycle that it's great to plan new projects, go on or explore the idea of a new adventure (no matter how small), or try a new hobby or recipe. To stay sparkly in this phase you'll need to mix life up a little. Think about trying things you've not done before because that's what your body and mind will naturally be wanting to do and this'll make you feel happier.

### Appetite

**Food:** Oestrogen has been known to have an appetite suppressing affect, so it's likely as this hormone rises in this phase you'll no longer have the same strong cravings and need for extra calories that can come on before and during your period. Lovely light foods like sparkly salads and more vitality-boosting veggies will make you feel energised and support your hormones in this phase. If you're not allergic to either, add into your daily diet 1 tablespoon of fresh ground flaxseeds (as this can help to get rid of excess oestrogen – which we don't want you to have) and 1 tablespoon of raw pumpkin seeds (because they're high in zinc which can support progesterone production).

**Sex:** This is a great time to add something new into your sex life because if you just engage in your 'normal' bedroom activities, you could be left feeling a little frustrated and bored by it all.

### Energy

Your follicular phase is straight after your period (when your energy has been at its lowest). So, don't try and do too much too soon or you'll easily exhaust yourself and not experience the lovely "lift" in energy and mood that should naturally occur at this time.

To be fully aligned with what your hormones are doing in this phase, it's a great idea to pick a sort of movement that's new and fun like roller-skating (you'll get to know what a fan I am of this past-time), hula-hooping, tap-dancing, having a kitchen disco, going for a jog somewhere you've never been before or changing up your normal dog-walking route. Sticking to the same type of movement routine day in, day out (as men tend to do to fit in with their hormones) will likely leave you feeling bored, uninspired, and unenthusiastic about moving your body at this point of your cycle.

If you're not currently doing any sort of movement to boost your sparkle, then this is the perfect time to gently start a new, sparkly habit – as you'll likely feel more up for it.

## Ovulatory Phase

*The second phase of your cycle.*

*Lasts approximately 3-5 days.*

## The sparkly season:

This phase can be likened to Summer. It's the time in your cycle when you're 'in bloom' and generally full of life and energy. This is naturally your most 'outward facing' or extroverted phase. If your hormones are balanced, you'll thrive and not feel worn out by socialising and being around other people – it's actually what your body *needs* in this phase to feel its best.

## The sparkly science:

Levels of FSH and LH rise acutely, which stimulate ovulation i.e. the follicle to release an egg into the fallopian tube. The egg will either be fertilised by a sperm or disintegrate on its way to the uterus. Both oestrogen and testosterone surge.

**What does this *actually* mean?**

**Mood**

You'll want to be around people and doing things. Communication and speaking up for yourself will be easier because oestrogen stimulates the parts of the brain associated with social and verbal interactions.

You'll feel more naturally upbeat and positive. You'll likely have a natural glow (fun fact: wearing rouge is actually meant to mimic the fertile and sexily flushed look from this phase). It's often around this time you'll feel most confident and happy with your looks as your skin will be plumper and eyes brighter. This is the phase you may feel a bit like a sexy, sparkly superwoman.

Your hormones create a natural magnetism and energy, literally drawing people to you in this phase (hence, it's when you're at your most fertile), so this is a good time to demand more for yourself at work or in relationships.

**Appetite**

**Food:** With the appetite suppressing effects of higher oestrogen, you'll likely enjoy your food but not feel ravenous or craving extra calories (like in the next two phases). This is a great time to add in extra fruits and veggies into your diet as well as a daily hot water with lemon or lime (unless you have stomach ulcers). This will all help support your liver and get rid of excess hormones that'll make you feel crappy if they stay in your body. If you're not allergic to either, add in daily 1 tablespoon of sunflower seeds (their selenium helps support liver detoxification and Vitamin E helps support healthy progesterone levels) and 1 tablespoon of sesame seeds (their high zinc levels help promote progesterone production).

**Sex:** Hell yes! If your hormones are working as they should, then this is the phase where your sex drive should naturally feel higher. Both the thought and activity of sex will usually be very welcome, appreciated, and sought out by your body.

### Energy

Your hormones will be giving you the energy and ability to 'go, go, go' without getting tired or burnt out. Enjoy being a social, sparkly, sassy, sexy woman. If you can, then this is the time to do work presentations, have important relationship chats, or arrange to see as many people as possible. If you're hormones are balanced, you can push yourself in every area in this phase without feeling depleted and crappy.

Just a word of warning. You'll likely be so excited by your super-boosted energy levels and interest in seeing people in this phase that you could contact an array of friends and say yes to various invitations that are planned for the next couple of weeks. This is a BIG mistake because in the next two phases of your cycle your energy will start dropping off and you'll naturally want more time alone and not to be around people.

Don't make plans in this phase of your cycle that you have to fulfil in the following weeks as your energy and appetite for socialising changes, sometimes dramatically. This is why one week you can't wait to meet up with your bestie and the next you don't want to leave the house for anyone.

Wherever possible, plan to do most of your socialising that requires a lot of energy and being around lots of people in your late follicular, ovulatory, and early luteal phases. This planning around your energy is vital if you want to stay as sparkly as you can throughout the month and not burnout.

Your body really needs movement in this phase of your cycle to get rid of any excess hormones and help keep them balanced. Your body will have extra energy to burn and intense workouts won't have a negative effect on your body or hormones. You shouldn't feel overly drained if you engage in things like running, cardio, circuits, HIIT or spin. At other times in your cycle this sort of exertion can cause your body to be more stressed, inflamed and imbalance your hormones, so don't get sucked into the masculine cycle of "feel the burn every day", because it's not best for your female body.

## Luteal Phase

*The third phase of your cycle.*

*Lasts approximately 10-14 days.*

### The sparkly season:

This phase can be likened to Autumn, a time when you gradually start slowing down and are getting ready for Winter (your menstrual phase), while still enjoying some of the benefits of Summer (your ovulatory phase). The start of this phase is 'outward facing' like your ovulatory phase but, it gently moves into being a more 'inward facing' and introverted season.

### The sparkly science:

Oestrogen, testosterone, and progesterone peak and then start to fall as you head towards your period. Your uterus lining (also known as the endometrium), composed of blood and cells, has been building up throughout the month to house a fertilised embryo, should there be one.

If you have oestrogen dominance (i.e. too much oestrogen in relation to progesterone in your body), then this is the phase you'll likely experience PMS – everything from feeling depressed, teary, and angry to having painful breasts, headaches, and bloating. Although PMS has been normalised by society and the medical profession because it's so common in women – you're not actually meant to suffer any of these symptoms. PMS is very normal but not necessary.

### What does this *actually* mean?

### Mood

Your 'happy hormone' (serotonin) levels drop in this phase (as your body gears up for menstruation) so you may feel less happy with your body, appearance, and life in general. Know that with regard to these feelings "this too shall pass". Understand that any exaggerated feelings of unhappiness are usually part of this hormonal shift and not a permanent state of being. You'll start to need more rest, reassurance, and crave time away from people.

The great part about this phase is your brain is wired to enjoy sorting things out and getting things done. Look to finish tasks at home or projects at work as this'll feel easier and super satisfying. That to-do list can decrease rapidly in this phase.

If you feel physically larger than usual in your luteal phase then it may be bloating from PMS. However, know that your uterus swells in size before and during your period. Don't use this as a reason to be down on your body size or shape. Think of this monthly expansion (where you may feel 'bigger' externally as well as internally) as a sort of pregnancy where a new version of you, along with a realigned purpose for your life, can be 'birthed' in the next phase when you have your period. It's time to speak lovingly to your body and literally give it some space. Ditch the skinny jeans and tight-fitting clothes – your uterus will thank you for it. I like to tell my clients when they feel this expansion before their period, "Give your womb some room!"

Remember your fluctuating female hormones mean you change physically and emotionally each month. You're not meant to rigidly try and stay the same weight or shape and panic if you're jeans are a little snug. Embrace the fact you have a 'moon cycle' and just as the tide goes in and out depending on what the moon is doing, so do you.

PMS symptoms in this phase (as well as a painful period in the next phase) indicates your hormones aren't as balanced as they should be, and you've not been looking after your mind and body as you should've throughout the previous month. However, if you reduce your inflammation (there's lots of info throughout this whole book to help you do that) and follow your body's changing needs throughout your cycle, PMS can genuinely be a thing of the past.

I'd never have believed this was true if it wasn't for the fact that I went from having the worst PMS out of everyone I knew – painful breasts, bloating, crying fits, and anger, to having no negative symptoms in the lead up to my period – just a slow decline in my energy and want to step back from being around people. Following the diet and lifestyle tips in this book should help you too be able to reduce or eliminate your PMS symptoms – which remember have been normalised but aren't necessary.

Whether you call it **PMT** or **PMS**, I want you to know that the minute you feel any PMS/PMT symptoms, you acknowledge that it's your body crying out **"P**ick **M**e **S**traightaway" (if you call it **PMS**) or **"P**ick **M**e **T**oday" (if you call it **PMT**). Don't continue to put the needs of others before your own when you feel these symptoms arise in your body. The minute you take action on this plea from your body and do some things that *you* want or need, you should start to see some of your symptoms reduce. It's kind of magical.

Oh, and if you need to cry in this phase – then please do! Let those tears flow, ask yourself what the real emotion or need is behind them and know those salty, sparkly sobs actually help rebalance your mind and body.

## Appetite

**Food:** You'll likely feel hungrier in the second half of this phase as your body prepares for the energy-intensive process of menstruation. Your body will need and want extra calories in this phase – it's not that you're being greedy or not having willpower (as the predominantly male-owned diet industry would have you believe).

Your body will likely want more carbohydrates for energy and comfort food cravings may increase e.g. foods with high fat, sugar, or salt, due to your serotonin levels dropping. To reduce your food intake in this phase would be like forcing a marathon runner to cut out carbs and reduce their calories before a big race. Listen to your body and its wisdom and simply eat more instead of berating it. Don't use this phase to start dieting, feeling crappy about eating too much, or cutting back on food.

Use your higher energy levels at the start of this phase to prepare the extra food that your body will ask you for in the second half of this phase – when your energy will be lower. You'll be more likely to pick super inflammatory foods as a fast option if you don't. Ideally, make sure you include some lovely carbs like sweet potatoes, butternut squash, some organic rice and ignore the diet speak that "carbs are bad".

I often prepare things like protein balls, a vegan chocolate cake, and some roasted chickpeas at the start of this phase that I can enjoy in the second half of this phase (and at the start of my period). I know I'll want more food but, I don't want to always be left grabbing junk food to satisfy my body's desire and need for those extra calories.

Enjoy nourishing your body and helping it to have the energy it needs before it has to shed the lining of your uterus. Add in lots of gorgeous greens and root veggies like spinach, cabbage, and beetroot to your meals to support your hormones and liver. Feel free to increase the amount of snacks you have (extra nuts, seeds or nut butter with fruit are great choices) so you don't get blood sugar crashes as these can affect your emotions. If you're not allergic to either, add in daily 1 tablespoon of raw sunflower seeds and 1 tablespoon of sesame seeds (for the same reasons as before).

**Sex:** You'll most likely go from still wanting sex in the first half of this phase to possibly wanting less in the second half – but just tune into your body and follow its prompts. The idea that women are often questioned, "How many times a week do you have sex" or given the idea that having a healthy sex life means engaging in it every day, shows once more that sex is too often focused on the male hormonal cycle. A woman's sexual landscape has a month to be fully explored and expressed – not a daily or weekly one.

As your body and brain chemistry changes and gears up for menstruation towards the end of this phase, you may crave more non-sexual intimacy, more communication, more encouragement/reassurance and have a greater need to express how you're feeling (if you struggle with this then you'll find tips in the 'Speak up for your Sparkle' chapter).

If you don't talk about what's on your mind and suppress your feelings in this phase, you'll likely feel ignored, misunderstood, full of pent up anger, and pretty sorry for yourself – hence why there are often more tears or arguments in this phase for women. The brain is the largest erogenous zone. Good communication and emotional intimacy is a big part of having a satisfying sex life, so don't skip it for the supposedly steamier stuff.

## Energy

In the first half of this phase, you'll still have the energy, horniness, and magnetism of the ovulatory phase, but as your hormone levels decline, your energy levels will, too. This decline can sometimes shock women as they ask "Why am I so tired this week, when last week I had so much energy?" It's your hormones! And perfectly natural, so you don't need to panic or just "push through". In the first half of this phase, you can pretty much carry on as you were in your ovulatory phase. However, as you get into the second half of this phase, you'll need 'no' to be your most used word. It's 'no' to unnecessary meetups, social activities, and extra work commitments. If you carry on with a 'go, go, go' instead of a 'no, no, no' mentality in this phase, you'll start to feel exhausted, overwhelmed, upset, cranky, and PMS symptoms will rage.

Gradually scale back from high energy movement (which is fine for the first half of this phase) to gentler forms of exercise (in the second half of this phase). Activities like Pilates (which I only started this year but love – mainly thanks to my wonderful teacher Tilly, who also teaches classes online if you want to join me. Go find her on Instagram @tillypilates), walking, and gentler forms of yoga should feel lovely at this time. Sweating in this phase can help ease some PMS symptoms – so consider using a sauna, taking an Epsom salt bath, or having the type of walk that makes your cheeks feel a little flushed.

## Menstrual Phase

*The final phase of your cycle, also known as your period.*

*Lasts approximately 3-7 days.*

## The sparkly season:

This can be likened to Winter, a season to hunker down, hibernate, get cosy, stay inside, snooze, rest, and reflect before Spring (your follicular phase) comes around again. This is naturally your most 'inward facing' or introverted season and means you'll likely feel happiest resting more and spending time on your own.

## The sparkly science:

Your hormone levels are at their lowest concentrations as your body goes through the physically taxing process of shedding the lining of your uterus. The left and right sides of your brain – the practical and the feeling sides – are the most connected in this phase (via a big bundle of nerve fibres). So you're literally 'wired' to be more analytical and intuitive with regard to what's going on in your life and around you.

### What does this *actually* mean?

### Mood

There's a negative stereotype of a woman on her period that we too often buy into. We often try and blame tears and mini meltdowns on it being that 'time of the month.' But actually, your hormone levels when you're on your period mean that your brain doesn't become more foggy or irrational. It actually becomes primed to work out the adjustments and solutions needed to improve your overall health, happiness, and sparkle for the month ahead. The tears and upset come when your wisdom nudges you to do this and shows you the things you're unhappy with, but you push your innate wisdom down and ignore it instead of addressing it.

This is a great time to journal how you're feeling about your life, relationships, and career and see how your womanly wisdom tries to reconnect you to your life's passions and purpose when your day to day life often keeps pulling you away from them. The key in this phase is simply to observe the things that come up for you and note them down. It's not the phase to start doing or changing things (this is what your next phase is for) as your energy will be low.

Your period is meant to be a time of rest and reset, not rage and resentment. Retreat, reflect, and take stock of how you're *really* doing and feeling. Let others take the wheel a bit here, don't just carry on trying to do it all – or you'll likely feel physically and emotionally terrible. Lavish yourself with self-care if you want to feel calm. Schedule in baths, early nights, a manicure or catch up on your favourite TV shows. Keep saying 'no' to people who want you to do stuff for or with them. Put your feet up more, even just for five minutes when you have your cup of tea or coffee.

Express your needs to those around you – cancel plans, ask for a shoulder rub, have someone buy you chocolate, ask someone else to cook. Start to normalise the fact that you have an energy-taking period and a small window of time that urges you to slow down and pause once a month. Wherever and however you can, get some extra help, support, and love at this time because you deserve it. If you have kids, ask your partner or a friend to look after them, even just for a few hours so you can have some space to rest and recuperate in this phase.

A question that's been used to try and humiliate, antagonise or belittle women experiencing higher levels of anxiety, anger, overwhelm or sadness has been "Is it your time of the month?" A phrase most women have hated to hear at one point or another. However, this was never meant to be a narky question used by others. It's actually a statement *you* should be stating to others when they continue to demand your time or energy. I want you to start declaring, "It's MY TIME of the month" i.e. your time to shed your uterine lining, rest, reflect, be left alone more and have others do things for you. This will leave you feeling calm, balanced, not exhausted and less like the male- created caricature of a woman on her period.

## Appetite

**Food:** At the start of your period you'll likely want to eat more, so do, and just enjoy it! Your body needs to be nourished and nurtured in this phase. Have a little of what you fancy guilt-free and treat yourself like an absolute Queen. Enjoy warming and comforting foods like scrumptious soups and add lots of veggies to your meals. Plan meals and batch cook ahead of time in your other phases so you have more time to rest in this phase. If you're not allergic to either, add in daily 1 tablespoon of fresh ground flaxseeds and 1 tablespoon of pumpkin seeds as this can support your oestrogen production and metabolism.

**Sex:** You'll be your most inwardly focused this week. Go with what your body is asking you to do with regard to sex. You'll need some time alone in this phase, so if you have a partner, tell them to make plans without you. Don't feel guilty about not wanting to be around your loved ones because having time apart is just as healthy as being together.

## Energy

Physically you'll have very little energy and reserves. Trying to carry on as normal, doing lots of activities, and being everything to everyone in this phase will have a negative impact on you physically and emotionally. Depression, breakdowns and feeling utterly overwhelmed, generally don't just appear out of nowhere in most women's lives. They usually come after years, sometimes decades of "cracking on" and taking no time to step back, rest, and reflect.

Most women are longing for a rest of some kind and nature knows this so has given you a time for it each month. Part of the role of your period and the lowering of your energy is to give you a brief pause once a month to make you slowdown, reduce the busyness, 'check in' with yourself, and find out how you're *really* feeling and what *your* needs are (as opposed to focusing on everyone else's). It's a time to use your analytical and intuitive brainpower that's ramped up so you can assess your health, career, relationships, and other important areas of your life.

So your body can recover from what it's doing and you can experience more energy in your next phase, you'll need to rest, rest, and rest some more. Oh, and did I say rest? So doing lots of movement at the start of your period? Nope, nada. The first two or three days particularly need to be a time of calm, low activity and, where possible, resting and naps so your body can restore its energy. I know you may say, "Naps would be a fine thing," but just try and take everything you're doing down a notch and ask others for help (did you know even a 6-12 minute rest with your eyes shut can be hugely restorative?). Towards the end of your period, you'll benefit from going for light walks and doing some gentle stretching, but nothing more strenuous or you'll just be releasing unnecessary stress hormones into your body.

Those adverts of women playing tennis, volleyball, and roller-skating during their period gives the message of 'just carry on as if nothing's happening'. In other words, ignore your period, be a man and keep the world running to a man's schedule and cycle! However, this is one of the most mentally and physically unhealthy things you can do to your body. You're not meant to ignore the fact that you are bleeding and just carry on as normal – it's why your menstrual blood is red – it's a 'stop sign' for your busy life.

Don't hide the fact you're on your period. Tell those closest to you and explain that your energy is lower. Acknowledge to yourself the physical gravity that having a period is. If you wouldn't expect a woman going into labour to keep doing everything she usually does, don't expect yourself to, either.

## Quick Recap

I know that understanding the four phases of the month is a huge amount of information to take in. You can refer back to the below lines to help you quickly work out what's happening with your energy, appetite, and mood (which are some of the main things that women feel they experience randomly, but actually experience cyclically) if your hormones are balanced.

**Follicular** – Your energy should be slowly increasing after your period. Your appetite and cravings should've reduced since your period. Your mood will likely be boosted by doing/eating/seeing new things and people. It's like **Spring.**

**Ovulatory** – Your energy should be at its highest. Your appetite should naturally be at its lowest. Your mood will likely be upbeat, energetic, and you'll be boosted by doing lots of things and seeing other people. It's like **Summer.**

**Luteal** – Your energy will stay high for the first part of this phase and then you should feel it gradually (or sometimes dramatically) decline. Your appetite will gradually or dramatically increase. Your mood will likely change from upbeat, energetic, and enjoying being around people to more introverted, detached, and needing alone time. It's like **Autumn.**

**Menstrual** – Your energy will likely be at its lowest and you'll feel tired. Your appetite will be moderately high and comfort foods will likely be craved. Your mood will likely be one of introspection and so you'll not want to be around other people. Rest will be what you need at this time. It's like **Winter.**

If you currently have a menstrual cycle, that's the four phases/seasons you go through every single month. Of course you can do anything at any time of the month, however, because of your cyclical nature, there are certain times during the month you'll just be more inclined or find certain things easier (in the same way men's hormonal shifts will make them find certain tasks easier or more natural than at other times in their 24-hour cycle).

You're not meant to do the same things with the same levels of productivity, energy, progress, and happiness day in day out. It's time to stop feeling like you're failing if you're not always producing things or feeling sexy, sociable, and full of energy every day. Having your sparkle as a woman isn't about always being outgoing, upbeat, and 'ovulatory' – which has wrongly been championed as the most valuable state for a woman to be.

No, being a woman with sparkle means you possess a kaleidoscope of emotions, experiences, and energy. Don't ever let someone stick a label on you or tell you that you should only be, feel, or even look a certain way to be worthy, wonderful, and whole. No season in your month or life is more valuable than another. I used to think I only had my sparkle when I was around people, making them laugh, being happy, and brimming with positivity. Now I know my value and importance doesn't waver when I'm needing to be alone, resting, ill, or upset. Each phase is needed, each phase is beautiful. You can sparkle in each phase.

Can I suggest at this point you download the MyFLO app by the period pioneer that is Alisa Vitti – it'll help you visually see your phases and has some wonderful information to help you optimise your cycle. I know it can be a bit overwhelming to start with, but stick with it. Learning about your phases is like driving a car or riding a bike, it'll soon become second nature to you and you'll love the freedom it brings. Start making some small adjustments each day to help yourself in each of your phases. I promise, this new way of living will boost your sparkle no end.

## Extra Powerful Period Info

Before we move on to some more sparkly science that relates to your hormones, I just wanted to give you some extra powerful period info because too many of us have grown up with the belief that it's gross, always has to be painful, and is something we should be ashamed of. The "diesease-ification" of women's normal bodily functions and hormonal shifts – be it putting a young woman on the pill for heavy periods (instead of trying to find out the reason for them first), making women feel panicked that they're in the perimenopause and suggesting anti-depressants (instead of explaining the full variety of options of support at this time) or ridiculing menopausal women and saying they've "dried up" – means women's belief that their bodies are strong, powerful, and healthy has been replaced by feeling like we're hormonal messes in constant need of doctors and drugs to regulate our symptoms, cycles, and selves.

Your female body and hormones are not against you. They're always working with you, in your favour, and leading you back to the path of health and happiness if you listen to and understand them. Your periods are an incredibly powerful part of that. A menstruating woman has been revered by many ancient traditions and societies, and this process used to be seen as divine – not disgusting. There's so much more to your periods than the modern negative narrative. Your periods can be a great indicator of what's going on in your overall health.

I believe that constantly getting rid of your periods or medicating your way through them (like I used to), isn't how you're meant to live as a woman. No matter what any textbook, person, or belief system has told you, periods aren't a curse to be endured with either mental or physical pain. They're in fact truly fascinating and can boost your mental and physical health if you work with them and understand their "language".

## Your Period Is Your Free Monthly Health Check-Up

Did you know that there are four 'vital signs' measured by doctors at health check-ups or in an emergency? Your heart rate, breathing rate, blood pressure, and temperature. These are all indicators for how well your body is functioning. However, the American College of Obstetrics and Gynecologists have said that your period is your $5^{th}$ vital sign. Your period is *so* important that it's now being recognised as a vital indicator of your overall short and long-term health as a woman.

This means that every single month, if you have a period, you're literally being given a health report by your own body as to how you're doing. If your period is painful, excessively heavy or light, changes, or disappears, it's one of your body's first signals to you that something needs addressing to bring it back into balance. You may be experiencing too much stress, not enough nourishment, have an excess or low levels of a vital hormone. To always wish our periods away or take medications to stop them means we're missing out on their monthly help for our health and wholeness. I believe we need to welcome the information our monthly bleed brings.

## Colour Coded

Did you know that you should take a look at the colour and consistency of your period? TMI? Look, I'd rather you know this stuff now and not get ill with a hormone-related disease like I did. So, let's stop being squeamish and start being sparkly scientists who understand our bodies.

A healthy period should normally be bright 'Christmas' red in colour with a consistency like runny honey. Any other colour could be a sign that something's not quite working as it should. If your period is brown, then this could mean you have old blood from your last period now coming out of your uterus, possibly indicating your progesterone levels are low. If your period is dark purple (typically with large clots), then this is often an indicator you could have too much oestrogen. Short-term this can produce not very fun symptoms like I had e.g. painful, exhausting, heavy periods. Long-term it could lead to more serious health problems. If your period's hardly there and very light pink, it could indicate that you may have too little oestrogen, often meaning your body's not getting the nutrients it needs from your diet. Start noticing the colour of your period so you can look to make some diet and lifestyle changes (like those suggested in this book) that could help prevent a health 'code red' situation in the future.

## Health-Boosting And Healing Blood

Have you noticed that menstrual blood is the only blood that the media and our culture has deemed 'disgusting' and generally isn't allowed to be shown or 'seen'? So much so that when it needs to appear in an advert for a sanitary towel or tampon, it's blue. Blue! In adverts for bleeding gums, the blood is red. In adverts for plasters for grazed knees, the blood is red. In fight scenes or when someone is violently killed on TV, it's red. But menstrual blood that's passed by over half the population at some point of their lives? Nope, that has to be blue. This only increases the shame and disgust that many women, especially younger girls, can feel about their periods. It reinforces the notion that our 5th vital sign should be hidden instead of normalised. Imagine being told to hide your pulse or breathing because those vital signs were deemed disgusting and shameful in society?

Guess what, though? Medical research is finally starting to catch up with the wisdom of ancient cultures who viewed menstrual blood as precious, powerful, and life-giving. So much so that it was often put onto the soil to fertilise it. What was once seen as a weird folklore tradition now makes scientific sense.

Research confirms that there's health-boosting and healing properties – in the form of stem cells – within menstrual blood. I won't go into too much detail, but stem cells are simply incredible because they can regenerate and repair damaged and diseased tissues in the body. This means they can be used in therapies to help people with things like cancer, Alzheimer's, Parkinson's, heart disease, arthritis, strokes and type 1 diabetes. The discovery of stem cells in menstrual blood means that this would currently be the only non-invasive way of collecting these precious cells from a woman (instead of via something like a bone marrow transplant). So, maybe women don't expel hideous, shameful, 'needs to be disguised as blue' blood. Maybe once a month women create and give out one of the most treasured, healing, and divine substances currently known to man and science.

## Hormonal Contraception

The subject of hormonal contraception and how the various methods affect you physically and mentally is too big for me to tackle here. However, there are plenty of other books and experts that can guide and inform you on this subject (I'll recommend some of my faves further down).

I want to just say quickly, I'm not opposed to hormonal contraception if it's your choice for your body. I am opposed however, to women being given a pharmaceutical drug (of any kind) that can alter how their mind and body works without being given all the information they need to make a truly informed decision with regards to their short term goals and long term health and happiness.

Whichever method of contraception you decide to use, please thoroughly research it first, find out what it does to your body and brain, how it works, what the most common side effects are and make sure it's 100% your choice. I believe it can only be *your* choice (as opposed to your doctor's or partner's) if you first understand your female cycle and second understand how hormonal contraception affects your whole mind, body, and cycle. To not understand how your hormonal contraception works in your body (and its possible adverse physical and mental side effects) would be like being recommended cigarettes as an appetite suppressant (which used to happen btw), without ever knowing or being told of the other ways cigarettes can negatively impact your overall health.

Hormonal contraception generally works by stopping ovulation from occurring in a woman's body*, and ovulation (when an egg is released from an ovary) doesn't happen in isolation. It's a full brain, body collaboration — so, these powerful medications don't just affect your ovaries and have been associated with a greater risk of depression and autoimmune disease compared with women who aren't on them. Many women on hormonal contraception go on to be prescribed anti-depressants.

A Danish study believed there to be a direct link between the two (especially in teenage and younger women). There's no shame or judgment with regards to being on hormonal contraception or anti-depressants. Both can be tools to help a woman when she's struggling or looking for solutions. However, it's worth noting that these are two of the most prescribed medications for women and both alter two of her most powerful functions – her menstrual cycle and her brain. I believe both of these medications can be used in the short term if that's what's wanted or desperately needed, but we must start to hear and help the deep cries of a woman's body and mind instead of always immediately silencing them. We must also listen to women who start these medications and intuitively feel they're not a good fit for them and have created new symptoms or not helped existing ones.

If it can be avoided, we ideally want to do all we can to not shut down ovulation in women's reproductive years (either through hormonal contraception or extreme dieting). Regular ovulation indicates that "all is well" and our bodies are getting the food they need and not experiencing excess stress. To think the process of ovulation and having a period (which remember is the 5th vital sign of womens health) can be chemically stopped for years with no mental or physical side effects is, I believe, naïve. The hormones created by ovulation are very much needed and help to build your health as a woman in the present, for pregnancy, and also in your peri and post-menopausal years. They're vital in helping to create your long-term health and can help prevent strokes, dementia, heart disease, and breast cancer.

Hormonal contraception is generally used in two ways for women, 1) As birth control to reduce a woman's chance of getting pregnant 2) As a medication given to women who are experiencing hormonal problems e.g. PMS, PCOS, heavy or irregular periods. I'm just going to give you some information which I believe you should know or think about if you're on or considering going on hormonal contraception:

## 1) For birth control – freedom for women or men?

- The contraceptive pill was originally meant to be for men. This makes great scientific sense seeing as men are the ones who are fertile 365 days a year, and women are only technically fertile for 24 hours once a month (although can get pregnant for approximately 3-6 days a month). I want you to just take a moment to let those numbers sink in because despite only being fertile for a maximum of approximately 6 days, it's women who are having their bodies and minds hormonally altered for 365 days of the year. Women are largely seen as the ones who should take responsibility for long-term contraception, despite men being the ones who are fertile all day, every day, all year.

- When a male contraceptive injection was trialled, the side effects of it – mood swings, acne, bloating, anxiety, depression, testicle shrinkage – caused men to leave the trial and the trial to be halted. These side effects were seen as unacceptable by and for men. It's these same side effects (although it's shrinkage of women's ovaries that can occur from hormonal contraception as opposed to testicles) that women can often suffer from, but are still encouraged that this is a great form of contraception for them to be on. But, for men, these life-altering side effects were seen as too great to continue to trial, produce, or market hormonal contraception for men.

- Hormonal contraception isn't a "light" medication that magically stops you having a baby and only affects your ovaries. It stops various signals from your brain reaching your ovaries and the synthetic hormones used affect every organ in your body – including changing your brain structure and function.

- The origins of hormonal contraception and it being tested on women without their consent or knowledge is beyond shocking and steeped in sexism and racism. I would encourage you to do an internet search on 'Racism, sexism and the pill' to find out how this medication wasn't originally based on a desire for women to experience sexual liberation. I believe the real freedom and liberation comes for women when men take on (or takeover, seeing as women have carried the burden for decades now) the responsibility of contraception.

Women can struggle physically and emotionally due to their choice of contraception but carry on with it because they don't understand what's happening to their bodies, the non-hormonal choices available, or more shockingly have partners who don't want to wear a condom, get a vasectomy, or take over the contraceptive burden.

Of course, it's more convenient for the entire male population if women continue to carry the burden and possible health complications of hormonal contraception. Men would likely reject the idea of having their testosterone "swiched off" until they wanted a baby so, I believe women shouldn't think stopping their ovulatory cycle is normal and no big deal. I think if we're striving for true equality in the world then let's not stop at the gender pay gap – let's look at the 'contraception gap' with women's short and long-term health being "paid less" due to important hormones not being made.

- Is hormonal contraception really progress for women or have we swapped the worry of generally pregnancy-free sex for having our beautiful hormones, bodies and minds altered? The first wave of women's sexual liberation came with being able to take 'the pill' and supposedly be "freed" from having unwanted pregnancies or periods. I believe the second wave of women's liberation should come with women being liberated from carrying the burden of contraception and enduring the body and brain disrupting effects that can come as part and parcel of that.

## 2) For hormonal imbalances – solution or suppression?

- Many women are put on hormonal contraception to 'regulate' their periods if their periods are heavy, painful, or irregular. It's seen as a "cure all" for many hormonal imbalances or problems and often dished out to women without a long consultation to find out why a woman's hormonal health is struggling. This truly horrifies me as it doesn't correct hormonal imbalances (as many women on it believe) – it merely masks them only for the problems to reappear, often more severely, once the medication is stopped.

- It increases inflammation in a woman's body and this therefore increases the risk of other problems and diseases in a woman's body.

- Most women who take the contraceptive pill believe they have a period each month when they bleed. They don't. It's their body having a "withdrawal bleed" from the synthetic hormones. The pill stops you ovulating and having a period, and it shocks me that many women don't know this, have not expressly been told and therefore not consented to this. They genuinely believe they're now experiencing "good periods" and have no idea their body has been put into a temporary menopause and their bleed is basically a fake period.

- Any hormonal imbalance in a woman must be looked at holistically. A woman's diet, lifestyle and stress levels should all be taken into consideration before the best course of action is decided upon. This can of course be done alongside a woman being given hormonal contraception, but should never be ignored because it could take too long or women are seen as "too complicated". Actually, as you'll see from the various recommendations in this book that have helped hundreds of women rebalance their hormones at any age, a balanced body with vibrant health is far easier for a woman to achieve than we've been led to believe.

Knowledge isn't only power, it's sparkle and health boosting so get ALL the knowledge you can on the good and bad stuff that can happen from your choice of contraception (or any other medication you're on) and never let a doctor dismiss you or your questions. Also, consider stopping letting a male partner shift the body and mind-altering burden of hormonal contraception onto you. If you're on or considering hormonal contraception for birth control or a hormonal imbalance, promise me you'll do more research on it than you do on which new car to buy or holiday to go on.

I highly recommend reading the book *Sweetening the Pill* by Holly Grigg-Spall (and listening to every podcast she's on) for more information on how women's health has been ignored when it comes to contraceptive choices. She's also producing a documentary with Ricki Lake and Abby Epstein called 'The Business of Birth Control' which is going to lift the lid on lots of information women haven't been freely given on this subject, so keep an eye out for that.

Other great books on this subject that may help you decide on contraception or help you balance your hormones naturally are *Womancode* by Alisa Vitti, *Beyond The Pill* by Dr Joelene Brighten, and also the *Period Repair Manual* by Dr Lara Briden (also check out her website www.larabriden.com for a whole host of help with women's hormonal problems and contraceptive choices).

*Some ovulation and natural cycling does occur on the hormonal IUD, but it can still produce many of the unwanted side effects of other hormonal contraception. Also, I was told this week that some doctors can get paid extra for women agreeing to go on certain types of contraception, so make sure you ask if this is the case if it's suggested you start a specific hormonal contraception for a hormonal problem.

### No periods? No problem.

Some women get so excited when they learn about the power of their female cycle for the first time. Then these women say to me, "But, I'm not having periods. So, what does this mean for me?" I want to reassure every single woman – whether you have periods or not, are in your reproductive years, transitioning out of them or way past them, you're still a cyclical goddess who should tap into and enjoy the benefits of living cyclically. Living cyclically is how the earth thrives and how you too can thrive as a woman at any age.

If you don't have a menstrual cycle to remind you that each month you should enjoy different seasons of both activity and rest; seeing people and time alone; creating new things and finishing up projects – you can acknowledge the gift that nature has given you and follow the Moon Cycle (some women refer to their menstrual cycle as this, too).

The 'men' in the words menarche, menstruation, and menopause comes from the Greek word 'men' meaning month and 'mene' meaning moon. Women have the moon to remind them how to live cyclically each month, just as men have the sun to remind them of their 24-hour cycle. As the moon travels around the Earth each month, it has different phases/ seasons, just like a woman. Sometimes the moon is a magnificent, blazing ball of light seen by all and sometimes it's totally hidden from sight and gives minimal light to others. The moon has an average 29.5 day cycle with 4 different phases, which beautifully mirrors the approximate length and phases of a woman's cycle.

As a woman, you're not separate from nature and its powerful rhythms and forces – you're intrinsically part of them and your whole health is affected by the earth's warmth, light, and movement. When you stop having periods (temporarily or permanently) you can look to live by or be inspired by your 'moon cycle'. Following the moon cycle can guide you through your phases, reminding you when you should shine brightly for all to see, and when you should take some time out, hide from the world (as much as you can), and recharge your sparkle. Your physical body and physical world interact with and impact one another. This is science to be taken seriously for your sparkle, not new age thinking to be dismissed as "woo woo".

**Here's how the 4 phases of the moon cycle mirror the 4 phases of the menstrual cycle** and can help you tune into your cyclical nature at any time or age. They are…

**The Full Moon** – when the moon is fully seen and illuminated in the sky. This full and bright ball of light can remind you to enjoy an 'outward' phase, like Summer or the ovulatory phase. You can benefit from the practices suggested in the ovulatory phase (described earlier), like increased socialising and feelings of sexiness, and more energetic activities.

**The New Moon** – when the moon is completely hidden from sight. The absence of light from the sky can remind you to enter an 'inward' phase, like Winter or the menstrual phase. You can benefit from the practices suggested in the menstrual phase (described earlier), like resting, reflecting, spending time alone and being cosy and quiet.

**The Waxing Moon** – when the moon is increasing in appearance again, in between the new and full moon. As the light of the moon increases, it can remind you that it's an 'outward' phase, like Spring or the follicular phase. You can benefit from the practices suggested in the follicular phase (described earlier), like taking up new hobbies or embarking on a new adventure, recipe or just spicing up your routine a little.

**The Waning Moon** – when the moon is decreasing in appearance, in between the full and new moon. As the light begins to fade, it can remind you that it's an 'inward', transitional phase, like Autumn or the luteal phase. You can benefit from the practices suggested in the luteal phase (described earlier), like completing tasks, getting things in order, and starting to gently slow down the pace of your life.

As you can see, whether you're not having periods for health, age or other reasons, your female cycle is embedded into the earth. I'd encourage all women to take some time daily (or get an app) to see what the moon is doing and reap the mental and physical benefits of following the guidance and reminders of the Moon Cycle.

## Perimenopause And Menopause – Hormonal Haywire Or Hormonal Rewire?

The perimenopause and menopause often get used interchangeably. As a woman, you should know the difference between them and what's going on in your body so you're not left feeling stranded and struggling, instead of sparkly. Here's a simple breakdown:

- **The perimenopause** or as I like to call it the **'Sparkly Shift',** is your transition between having periods and not having periods. Your reproductive hormones slowly begin to shift and this leads you to the point where you no longer ovulate. This process can take anything between 5 and 20 years (although the average is 5-13 years).

- If you no longer ovulate, you no longer have periods. When you haven't had a period for a year and you're in the right age bracket of around 45-58 then, it's likely you have gone through or will be "diagnosed" as having gone through **the menopause** – or as I like to call it your **'Freedom Years Full of Sparkle'.**

### The Sparkly Shift

The perimenopause seems to be the latest "disease" that's been inserted into a woman's hormonal timeline that she's been told to dread and worry about. The lack of knowledge and mystery around this time often only increases a woman's anxiety and fear of it. The perimenopause is banded about as a reason the minute a woman starts experiencing any kind of negative hormonal issues in her 40's.

It's often when women are encouraged to be patched-up or propped up by hormonal contraception or other medications so as not to experience or suffer from the symptoms that can be present at this time. However, your perimenopause should ideally be no more dramatic or need to be medically assisted than your pre-menarche years i.e. the years that lead up to your first period.

If you have worked on keeping inflammation down and your hormones balanced in your reproductive years then there's no reason for you to experience a horrific perimenopause as opposed to a wonderful Sparkly Shift.

**The Sparkly Science**

Here's a simplified version of what's going on in your body during this time:

- There's a shift in your reproductive hormones. This should happen quite slowly and steadily if your hormones are balanced and your inflammation low.
- Progesterone (which is the hormone that among other things produces a calming, anti-anxiety and anti-insomnia effect on you) is the main hormone that declines during the Sparkly Shift. Much of the help given to women during the Sparkly Shift can wrongly be based on the theory that this time (and therefore the

symptoms experienced) are caused by oestrogen deficiency.

- Oestrogen during your Sparkly Shift can stay stable, increase, or fluctuate.
- Testosterone can start to decline.
- Your adrenal glands (also known as the 'stress glands') begin to pick up the production of your sex hormones that your ovaries are beginning to slow or stop.

**Possible Symptoms**

Some women have really horrible symptoms during this time and other women literally sparkle the whole way through this transition. Hormonal imbalances can appear or increase during your Sparkly Shift, but you must understand a crappy time and health challenges aren't a given that you have no control over, they're usually always linked to your diet, thoughts, and lifestyle.

- You'll often notice a change in your periods during the Sparkly Shift – they may increase or decrease in regularity, flow and/or pain.

- Negative symptoms that can be experienced during this time are generally the same as what you experience with

PMS – mood swings; weepiness; irritability; bloating and/or weight gain; migraines; hazy thinking, hot flashes etc.

- If you experience PMS symptoms in the luteal phase of your menstrual cycle, it's usually due to inflammation. This then creates a hormonal imbalance, namely too much oestrogen and it's this excess of oestrogen that gives you crappy symptoms. This inflammation, hormonal imbalance and crappy symptoms is the same pattern that occurs during your Sparkly Shift and your declining progesterone can make it worse. But, just like with your menstrual cycle PMS, there are many things you can do to reduce inflammation and rebalance your body. The same is true during your Sparkly Shift.

- Some women experience a decreased sex drive, loss of/thinning pubic hair, depression and this can be from either a decline in testosterone, too much stress, or a general unhappiness with their life (the 'Sexy Sparkle' chapter can help you with this).

**Sparkly Solutions**

During the Sparkly Shift, if women struggle with life-interrupting symptoms, many are once again dismissed, told it's normal "women's problems" and should be expected once you hit your 40's. The most common 'fixes' offered are synthetic hormones, bio-identical hormones, hormonal contraception and/or anti-depressants. Women should always be free to use these medications to make them feel better but, I believe not without help and understanding as to what the root cause of their symptoms are because it's never a one size fits all. For one woman her inflammation, oestrogen dominance, and horrible symptoms may be caused by the stress of a divorce or unhappy relationship. For another it could be her diet. For another it could be using too many products containing hormone disrupting chemicals. Discovering the root cause of your personal inflammation and imbalance can not only help reduce or get rid of unwanted symptoms, it can more importantly protect you from other unwanted and more serious health conditions.

When going through the 'The Sparkly Shift', there's always two areas that you should look at 1) The physical and 2) The emotional/spiritual.

## 1) The physical

The big thing to understand is the same chronic inflammation and hormonal imbalance that can cause a woman to struggle with heavy periods, PCOS, fibroids, PMS etc in her reproductive years is the same fuel lighting the fire of any perimenopausal symptoms that flare up. Often those symptoms or problems have been ignored, suppressed (with hormonal contraception or medication) and not addressed in the previous years or decades. This means this new hormonal shift can add gasoline to the fire of those previous symptoms. This is a time when women must look to reduce the levels of inflammation in their bodies. Sadly, these tend to be the years that women increase them, with extra stress from family and work responsibilties, more sugar, alcohol, dairy, too little rest, anti-inflammatory foods and water.

It may seem like one of the hardest things to do during these years, but reducing your stress levels is THE most important thing a woman can do to help her hormonal health during the Sparkly Shift (and before). The reason being is that as your ovaries decide it's time to start thinking about having a well-earned rest and go into part-time as opposed to full-time work, your adrenal glands pick up the ovaries shifts for secreting progesterone, oestrogen, and testosterone. However, by the time a woman's in her 40's, she's normally so stressed from her work, diet, and lifestyle that her adrenal glands focus on producing the stress hormone cortisol instead of all the sparkly sex hormones that help make a woman feel fab.

The result – increased crappy symptoms and feeling as if you have zero sparkle. The solution? Do all you can to decrease the things that stress your body in your life, diet, and environment. The following chapters of this book will take you through many of the ways you can reduce your stress, inflammation, balance your hormones and have a happier, healthier, more sparkly life wherever you are on your hormonal journey.

**2) The emotional/spiritual**

The perimenopausal years are essentially a mirror image of adolescence in which externally and internally a woman's hormones are shifting as she's transitioning from one stage of her life to the next. It's again similar to adolescence because it's when a woman's body and mind are urging her to "break free" from the path or person she thinks she should be, has been told to be, or has become due to the pressures of the world and those around her. It's a time when a woman is being nudged to find her way back to who she was created to be. Women can often believe that this is a time of betrayal by their bodies, but it's the opposite. It's your body refusing to be silenced until you face up to and improve the quality of your life and health.

The more you plug back into your true self and make little or big, serious or fun changes, the more health, vitality, and sparkle you'll see during this time. For me it's included trusting in myself more instead of always outsourcing my approval to others. It's disagreeing with many of the mainstream teachings of the organised religion I was brought up with that told me from birth I was wrong, broken, and should try to be someone other than myself to please God. I now believe that from birth I was full of sparkle and light and can only fulfil my God-given purpose by being my most true self i.e who God created me to be, not what religion told me I should be.

It's meant instead of being worried about being "too sparkly" and not being taken seriously in my business, I'm even more sparkly. It's meant instead of trying to find clothes that are flattering or make me look desirable to others, I focus on being desirable to myself and not wearing anything I have to hold my tummy in for. It's made me say "no" to so many things I would have said "yes" (and not wanted to) before. I'm loving the changes of the Sparkly Shift as I grow in confidence, untether myself more and more from society's or other's expectations and demands of me, and find my way back to my true self.

A dear friend of mine who's also about to begin to embark on her Sparkly Shift messaged me today because she's had her nose pierced. She sent me a picture of it saying, "I've been wanting to do this for ages. I had it when I was younger but then I started becoming a 'good girl' and took it out. For too long I've been in a little box of other people's approval and I'm bloody done with it…" This is the sass, strength, and sexiness of The Sparkly Shift I'm talking about! It's time to find that teenage rebel within you who decides that now is the time for a little more fearlessness, fun, and freedom not feeling constantly tired, fraught, and frumpy.

**Freedom Years Full Of Sparkle**

I want you to understand that the perimenopause and the menopause are hugely significant both spiritually and emotionally – just as your first period was meant to be. You're being led into exciting new chapters of your life as a woman, not closing the book on youthfulness, fun, and happiness. If you take care of yourself, your hormones, and honour your emotional needs, then this stage of your life can actually be a time where your sparkle is boosted, not battered. Take note. Just like your periods, the menopause or your 'Freedom Years Full of Sparkle' has had some pretty crappy PR for decades.

So, what's *your* view of the menopause and post-menopausal years? Do you think it's a happy, vibrant time in a woman's life? Do you think of a woman described as 'post-menopausal' as sassy, sexy, sparkly, and about to embark on what could be the most adventurous chapter of her life? Do you think of the menopause as a spiritual (not just physical) event where a woman can move away from her past and enter a time of rebirth, rejuvenation, and reinvention? No? Funny that. The media and some medical institutions have done a great job at suppressing and subverting the experience of the menopause so that it's become something women dread and are ashamed of rather than welcome (oh look, it's the same message we've had about our periods and the perimenopause).

When you hear the word 'menopause', you probably immediately think of hot flashes, weight gain, low libido, irrational behavior, and the end of any youthfulness as a woman. And you may think of a woman who's gone through the menopause as someone who's dowdy, miserable, 'dried-up', and not fabulous at all. But, it was never meant to be like this! In the same way your periods and perimenopause were never meant to painful, dreadful, and shameful, the menopause was never meant to signal the end of a woman's sparkle, vibrancy, and vitality. It was *always* meant to signal the start of a new version of it. It was meant to be your body's final period fanfare, announcing the arrival of an incredible new season in a woman's life that's full of sparkly freedom.

## The Sparkly Science

- Did you know that in your Freedom Years Full Of Sparkle your hormone levels go back to what they were roughly before you started your periods? They're similar to one of the most youthful times in your life. This means your body and brain is primed in the same youthful way it was when you likely had big dreams, less responsibilities, less cares, less insecurities, and didn't feel the need to be serious or responsible for others health and happiness all the time. Your hormones pre-periods weren't nudging you to always nurture others and you'll likely have had more hope, fun, dreams, and expectancy for your life. This can and should return to you in full force after you've gone through the menopause (or if you didn't have a great time in your younger years for whatever reason, this is the time you can get to experience that fun and freedom).

- You still produce around 40-50% of the oestrogen you did in your reproductive years, so, it's not true that your oestrogen disappears and that you "dry up" – as is the caricature of a woman who's gone through the menopause.

- Your follicle-stimulating hormone (FSH) and luteinising hormone (LH) levels – which when you're having a menstrual cycle rise to trigger ovulation and then decrease again – no longer fluctuate like they did in your reproductive years. They remain at the same, steady elevated levels for the rest of your life. The reason this so interesting and exciting with regards to your sparkle is because it's your ovulatory phase when you generally feel the most confident, happy, sexy, energised, and fabulous as a woman! The ovulatory (Summer) energy which previously would drop off as you headed into your luteal (Autumn) and menstrual (Winter) phases now stays with you for good.

The other interesting thing about your FSH and LH remaining at the levels they would during ovulation is that this is when you're naturally most biologically fertile. This energy, magnetism, and fertility in you as a woman (which before was subject to hormonal fluctuations) is now constant and uninterrupted. Your fertility hasn't ended because you can no longer conceive children. It's just shifted into you conceiving and birthing a whole array of other wonderful things into your life and this world.

Also, just to say, as a woman don't ever let anyone label you as 'infertile' at any stage of your life because not being able to have children might be a medical diagnosis but your fertility as a woman exists regardless. You must know that your body and mind are always able to create, grow, and birth incredible things into this world should you choose to.

## Possible Symptoms

- Women who've gone through the menopause can suffer from low oestrogen-related problems which can include more frequent UTI's and infections of the vagina, night sweats, headaches, dizziness, and vaginal dryness. Remember it's your adrenals that take over the heavy-lifting of oestrogen production, so it's usually because you're experiencing too much stress as opposed to you being a 'menopausal woman' with all the expected symptoms.

- If you've gone through an artificial menopause (due to the removal of your ovaries, the taking of certain drugs, chemo or radiotherapy) then your hormone levels drop instantly as opposed to a slower decline during the Sparkly Shift. This can make any symptoms experienced more severe. Premature menopause (going through it in your early 30's or 40's), is usually associated with chronic stress, excessive exercise, or autoimmune problems and can comes on suddenly making symptoms seem more overwhelming. A natural menopause in women with one or both her ovaries often produces more gradually occurring symptoms.

## Sparkly Solutions

Stress and the shackles of constantly looking after others must be reduced during this time of your life – it's what your hormones are demanding. When you menstruate, your hormones naturally wire you to nurture and mother others. It may be children, a job or business, pets, parents, or friends. However, the end of your periods signifies a shift – it's nature's nod to take your foot off the nurturing pedal and put the focus firmly back onto you. It's time to nurture and mother yourself back to your full health and potential. The end of your periods doesn't signal the end of your worth or value in this world.  It signals the start of a new journey. A journey that's not meant to be about spending all your free time looking after your grandchildren or elderly parents, but it's meant to be a time focused (at least some of the time) on you.

Can you imagine that? A phase of your life as a woman that's about you – *your* health, *your* happiness, *your* hopes, *your* dreams, *your* desires, *your* appetites, the things that are convenient for *you*! The things that make *you* feel fabulous, joyful, sexy, and sparkly! The menopause is meant to be your rebirth and not your death. It's meant to be a time when your sparkle can burn brighter, not burn out. Want to know why there can be an increase in anger and rage during this time? It's because many women don't or won't give up caring for others as their priority. They no longer have the hormones to support this lifestyle and so their body and mind rages that they're still working for others when the wisdom of their inner soul continues to ask them to work on themselves now.

Your soul is calling you back to your true self more than ever at this time, especially if you've spent a lifetime moving further away from it. If your body continues to just serve others, then a mental and physical war within you can ensue. If self-care, self-reflection, and taking action on doing things for you doesn't happen, then the symptoms many women get are heat-based like hot flashes and night sweats. Take that heat as a sign your body is angry at you not listening to it and ignoring your own needs. Let that heat and rage direct you to a life that suits you more, not others. A study was conducted to see if meditation (not medication) reduced hot flashes and the results were astounding. It reduced them in 90% of women in the study. A sure sign that taking time for yourself, calming your body and mind and tuning into your body can reduce unwanted symptoms for many women. However, lots of women don't want to or are scared to take time for themselves, stand up for themselves, and move out of the roles that others benefit from them being in. They never practiced taking this 'me time' time during their periods and so it can feel alien, unnatural and utterly selfish.

Acknowledge that because your hormones have shifted, your brain chemistry has too and even 'senior moments' that occur after the menopause (or sometimes in the perimenopause too) that are assumed to be brain degeneration, are often a signal of your brain chemistry shifting, upgrading, and moving your thinking from the logical left part of your brain and into the more creative, right side of your brain. This shift is meant to make you less worried about all the silly details that previously stressed you out.

In this new phase of your life, the multitude of minor things that filled your days should matter less. So, if you forgot to buy the loo roll or milk that your family asked you for, instead of panicking and rushing back out, you're meant to have a "Who cares?" attitude and head off to your salsa or life-drawing class. You must remind yourself during this time that you're not mentally "losing it". You're losing old ways that no longer serve you. You're no longer everyone else's servant. It's time to be a Queen, serve yourself and increase your sparkle.

Your Freedom Years Full of Sparkle are when you should tap into your youthful and carefree ways of living, feeling, and thinking as a free-spirited woman. You should care for and nourish your body, mind, and spirit like never before. You should open up to and follow the deepest callings and longings of your soul and you'll see your health and sparkle soar.

## It's All Linked

The secret to having the best 'Sparkly Shift' and 'Freedom Years Full of Sparkle', without going through all the stereotypical symptoms you've been told about, are pretty much the same things you need to do to have a great menstrual cycle without crazy symptoms. You have to make some diet and lifestyle changes that help reduce inflammation in your body and balance your hormones. You also have to develop a new rhythm of life that reflects your original, cyclical nature as a woman. You have to not ignore your body and its needs.

Women who have PMS, painful periods, and other hormonal problems often go on to have some of the worst perimenopausal and menopausal experiences. You see it's all linked. So, don't just put up with crappy periods only to have a crappy perimenopause and menopause. Do all you can now. Follow some of the advice in this book to reduce your inflammation and help balance your body and mind (or work with a recommended holistic therapist to help you do this), so you can embrace the transition to the perimenopause and menopause as the liberating time of creativity, vitality, and fun that it was always meant to be.

Every hormonal phase of your life is your body rewiring and giving you a sparkly system upgrade, not the hormonal haywire and downgrade we women have long believed or been taught. In the same way women aren't taught the power, positivity and benefits of their menstrual cycles, the same happens with regard to the hormonal transitions of their Sparkly Shift and Freedom Years Full Of Sparkle. Let's start to change that for the women growing up behind us. Let's embrace all our hormonal phases and shifts, knowing there's immense power, beauty and sparkle in them all.

## You Made It!

Phew! That was a lot of sparkly info, I know. I believe this is some of the most interesting, informative, and important science-based stuff for you to know about your body. If you want to learn more about your cycle, then there's suggested resources in the 'Sparkly Recommendations' section. Alisa Vitti, Dr Christiane Northrup, Dr Joelene Brighten, and Lara Briden are all huge pioneers in this area and I cannot thank them or recommend their books, courses or websites enough.

If you're struggling with your hormones, can I ask that like my clients you invest in your health and work with someone to get your periods pain-free and regular? If this isn't possible at this time then follow the tips in this book, look at my or other's courses, and read other books on this subject. Please know that having good periods and enjoying hormonal balance is possible. If I hadn't had such a dramatic change in my own life, from horrific to happy, I'd never have believed this was achievable. So many of my clients too have all gone from unbearable periods ruining a big portion of their lives, to them simply being a normal, no-drama part of their month. I want the same for you. Don't let something that happens every month for about 40 years of your life stop you from being happy, feeling wonderful, and getting your sparkle back.

### 1 small sparkly step for today...

So, my darling sparkle sister, can I ask you begin to get to know your body a little better, work with your menstrual and/or moon cycle, and get excited that your health is in your hands not someone else's? This is one of the most important things that'll help you start to grow in health, glow from within, and get your sparkle back.

If you're having periods, then download the MyFLO App to help track your cycle. If you're not having periods, then find an app that tells you what phase the moon is in (in the country you live in) so that you can start to follow that. If you prefer a more manual method, then get a notebook and pen, write down the day of your cycle (day 1 is the first day you start bleeding) or day 1 of the month if you're not having periods, and note your mood, energy, and appetite. Do this every day for a few months and then see if you start noticing what cyclical patterns are emerging.

# SUPER SPARKLY HAPPY HORMONES

Let's now look to tackle the next piece of your sparkle puzzle – chronic inflammation. Inflammation is basically your body's response to anything that's not good for you that you come into contact with. Short term (i.e. acute) inflammation – like the redness that occurs around a cut, the swelling after hitting your head, or the rash from a nettle sting is your body's healthy, natural, and pretty incredible defense and healing system. However, long-term (i.e. chronic), cellular inflammation that's a constant presence in your body (like a dripping tap) is something we want to reduce for your best health and sparkle. It doesn't just throw off your hormones and give you crappy symptoms, it's the root cause of most long-term degenerative diseases, cancers, accelerated ageing, and a whole host of other things that can steal your vitality and life. I believe being proactive at reducing chronic inflammation and bringing your hormones back into balance through some simple diet and lifestyle changes (like the ones covered in this book), can not only help you get your sparkle back, but secure and keep it too.

## Uninvited, Drunk Guests Ruin A Happy Party

Before I give you some of my top tips for reducing inflammation, I want to try explaining the terms 'chronic inflammation' and 'hormonal imbalance' and show you how they relate to each other. I believe that when we understand these two things and learn how to best avoid or minimise them, we can super-boost our mental and physical health and skyrocket our sparkle. Yes, our bodies are complex and utter miracles in their intricacies and design. But, the way we can keep our bodies in health and balance are relatively simple and don't always need complex solutions or medications. I want women to have more understanding about their bodies and some of the most common reasons for how and why they can go wrong. I want the power of their health in women's hands so they don't have to always feel so mystified by various symptoms or reliant on (and sadly often let down by) medical professionals or short-term, superficial, solutions.

I'm guessing that for years you (or those around you) have been blaming your PMS, mood swings, acne, and sugar cravings on your hormones without actually knowing what they are or do. Well, your hormones are kind of a big deal as they (along with your neurotransmitters) control your body and emotions. Hormones are chemical messages carried in your blood from glands like your ovaries, pancreas, and thyroid to your brain and other organs. These hormonal "messages" give your brain and other organs instructions on what to do.

Your hormones control every function in your body. They dictate things like whether you feel hot or cold, sleepy, stressed, hungry, horny, happy, have a period or get pregnant.

When they're in balance, it's like your body is playing a beautiful symphony for you to dance to and live by. Yet, when they're out of balance (because you have too much or too little of any of them), they can cause horrible gong-like 'clanging' and often life-disrupting symptoms.

If you can, think of having a healthy body as being like a beautiful, elegant, summer garden party. Your hormones are basically the super-efficient event organisers of this party and in charge of giving orders to all the other 'staff' (i.e. your organs). Their job is to keep everything running smoothly, happily, and on time. When everyone is doing their job properly then you have a lovely time.

Now, let's talk about the peskiness that is chronic (ongoing/long-term) inflammation because every woman I work with seems to be struggling with this in one form or another. Remember, inflammation is your body's response to anything that isn't good for you – be it deep fried food, an insect bite, or unrelenting stress. Chronic inflammation, which can result in anything from eczema, arthritis, painful periods to cancers, is caused primarily by things in your diet and lifestyle. The good news is though - you can largely control these things. Constant stress, too much sugar, trans fats (I'll explain more about these in a bit), and alcohol are just some of the real baddies for your body. They can all cause inflammation and stop your brain and body being able to have the correct

97

hormonal 'conversations' that enable it work well and stay in vibrant health. There's generally no problem (unless our health is already severely compromised) in having some of these things some of the time. However, too many people are ingesting all of these things, a lot of the time.

So, let's go back to a healthy body being like a perfect summer garden party. Your hormones are being the ever-efficient, instruction-giving event organisers keeping all the staff doing their jobs wonderfully so that music is playing, drinks are flowing, and food is being served. Well, inflammation is like a mob of drunk, rowdy, uninvited guests who disrupt and ruin everything. This 'raucous' inflammation inserts itself in between the event organisers (your hormones) and the various staff members (your body's organs) meaning your hormones can't be 'heard' correctly by the various parts of your body that need their vital instructions on how to function properly. The event organisers instructions go unheard or misheard and the previously happy, harmonious party is no longer smooth-sailing.

Your body is wonderfully designed to be able to reduce short-term inflammation. One or two drunk guests at your summer garden party of health can easily be dealt with by your full-time security guards (i.e. your immune system). However, chronic inflammation – which would be like a group of 100 drunk, disruptive and uninvited guests refusing to leave and causing fights for hours on end – is too much for your body's immune system (security guards) to cope with and not what they were originally employed to do. Now you can "beef up" your security by adding anti-inflammatory foods, drinks and practices into your life, but your body needs to be able to have a break from always having to constantly fight inflammation from certain foods or other stressors. You don't want your body exhausting itself by having to constantly fight the 'fires' of unnecessary inflammation instead of doing things like creating vibrant energy, repairing, or creating new healthy cells.

If you have high and constant levels of inflammation in your body, you won't get to experience the level of health and sparkle that's possible for you. Just as happened to me, you could experience and suffer with a variety of physical and mental problems be it painful periods, skin issues or more serious things. New research and studies are also showing that people who experience ongoing anxiety and depression are likely to have some form of chronic inflammation which should always be addressed alongside anything else that's being done to help the condition. It's why a pro-sparkle and anti-inflammatory diet and lifestyle is so important for all of us to aim for if we want more (not less) health and happiness as we age.

## What Goes Up, Must Come Down

The great news is you have so much power over chronic inflammation and being able to minimise or off-set the damage it does to your beautiful body. For example, if you're going through an unavoidably stressful time at work or in life (which happens to us all) – this would cause ongoing inflammation in your body. However, you can look to make the things you eat or do less inflammatory. This can look like trying to eat more colourful fruits and veggies, reducing things like sugar, dairy, and alcohol, resting more, or getting out in nature as much as possible. Likewise, if you're consuming foods and drinks that cause inflammation to your body, then you can try and help your body out by thinking grateful, positive, and uplifting thoughts while you're having them, instead of being stressed, angry or feeling guilty. You could also include playing mood-boosting music, laughing or doing some form of movement in your day to all help signal to your body that although it's ingested some things that have caused inflammation, it's safe and well.

I love telling my clients how they can bring balance back to what can feel like the see-saw of their health and be empowered by their daily lifestyle and eating choices. Once they start to learn which habits, foods and drinks are inflammatory and which are anti-inflammatory, they can start to off-set the bad ones and increase the good ones. It's simple maths. For instance, something like a doughnut will increase the inflammation in your body. However, if you then eat a cup of anti-inflammatory foods like blueberries or strawberries, you can help bring that inflammation down pretty quickly to help minimise the negative effects on your body.

I enjoy cake – which is not great news for my inflammation levels however, as often as I can, I'll add something anti-inflammatory to my plate as well, like some dark-coloured berries. Or if I know in the evening I'll be having an inflammation-causing takeaway (most are due to the crappy fats they're cooked in, plus the added sugar and dairy), then for my breakfast and lunch I'll focus on having foods and drinks full of anti-inflammatory goodness. If I'm eating it at home, I'll often even add a side of broccoli or rocket to my takeaway to help my body out. Why not do your own sparkly research on all the wonderful anti-inflammatory foods, drinks, herbs, and spices that nature has given us and think about including them to "sparkle-up" as many of your meals/ snacks/drinks as possible.

I see it as "what goes up, must come down". The more I know a food, drink, situation or emotion can increase my body's inflammation through chemicals, sugar, being heavily processed or stress, I want to do all I can to reduce it as soon as possible. I see inflammation as being like an internal fire that's been started inside my body. If there was a fire on the outside of my body, I'd get water to put it out and ice to cool it immediately. So, I don't want to leave the internal fires of inflammation burning away so it becomes chronic and could produce horrible hormonal symptoms or other diseases. I want to put it out or "cool" it as soon as I can.

Before I dive into sharing the info on some of the things that can increase or decrease inflammation and therefore bring increased health, hormonal happiness or horrible symptoms – there's 3 things **I want you to remember:**

1) **We're all different.** Before I start telling you about some foods and drinks that can make you feel better by reducing your inflammation, helping to balance your hormones, and boost your energy, let me quickly tell you about something called 'bio-individuality'. Bio-individuality is just a fancy, schmancy way of saying you my darling, are a total one-off.

The unique way your body processes and responds to various things in your diet (and environment) isn't often talked about. It's vital that you understand and be empowered by this concept. It means that how you react to various foods, drinks, and lifestyle practices will affect you differently from the next person, even if you're related to them. It's why your friend may be able to happily eat bread and pasta with no adverse effects, but it makes you feel lethargic, bloated, and foggy-headed. Or why one woman (i.e. me) can feel jittery, get heart palpitations, feel nauseous, and can't sleep properly after one cup of coffee. While others can happily drink several espressos and sleep like a baby that night.

You see, despite what you've been told or sold, there's no cookie-cutter, 'one-size fits all' plan for you in terms of food and drinks. Yes, you can be given information about certain foods and drinks and how they generally affect your body, but it's you who must do the ongoing work of tuning in and listening to your body's feedback after everything you eat or drink. In other words, *you* have the power to know what's best for your body, energy, and sparkle.

No doctor, scientist, specialist, celebrity, or sparkly woman who's written a book (as fabulous as she may be), will ever beat the knowledge and knowing you have about your own body. Whether you're aware of it or not, your body gives you feedback on a daily, hourly, even moment to moment basis about what boosts and what reduces its sparkle. Tune in to your body today and ask – do you feel better or worse after you've eaten a certain thing? Do you have more or less energy in the hours after eating/drinking something? Do you feel nicely full or horribly bloated?

Start taking note of the things that make you feel good mentally and physically compared to the things that make you feel crappy and lethargic – then simply adjust your habits accordingly.

2) **I want you to be free**. I used to think that being free meant that I could eat and drink whatever I wanted, whenever I wanted – I then got seriously ill (mainly due to my diet and lifestyle) and illness feels like the opposite of freedom if you ask me. I then thought that being free (mainly from disease) was banning myself from eating anything that harmed my body by causing inflammation and hormonal imbalances. I now realise that true freedom comes from me knowing about the potential effect something has or can have on my body. Then, with that information, deciding what I want to do depending on the way I want to feel and the things I want to achieve in my life. If I understand how something affects my body, then if it's negative, I have the opportunity to balance out what's happening physically and emotionally to protect my health and sparkle. That personal power and autonomy over my

health feels like true freedom to me and I want the same for you.

3) **Things change.** Life doesn't stay the same. At some points in our lives we're able to make choices with our highest health goals in mind (and if we're seriously ill, this should always be a priority). At other times, for whatever reason, we can't and that has to be okay. I never want you to box yourself in a corner and say, "I'm quitting sugar forever," only for you to experience guilt when after a sleep deprived week you grab some biscuits to get you through a tough day. I don't want you to decide to become tee-total only for you to be at a wedding and wish you could have a glass of champagne to toast your friends happy day (I'm obviously giving this advice for people who don't have a problem with or dependency on alcohol). Allow yourself freedom and flexibility in life. Always try to make the best choices for your own body and health, but in the times or situations you can't, just relax (because relaxing reduces stress in your body, which reduces inflammation – yippee!).

I know not every woman can work with someone like me to boost their sparkle by helping them find the root cause of their problems, reduce their inflammation, and help balance their hormones. So, I want to arm you with the information that I believe can empower you and help to boost your health, vitality, and sparkle. This information is what I give to most of my clients and now you get to have it too.

It wasn't until I was in my 30's that I realised the things I'd been struggling with in my health could've been helped (or hindered) by what I was eating and drinking daily. I was unknowingly choosing with every food or drink to boost or reduce my health. I'd previously always thought that my only hope for fixing my health and hormones came through a doctor, pill, or operation. I'd even been told by doctors that my bad skin, terrible periods, and breast tumour had nothing to do with my diet – which I now know is simply not true. My diet wasn't the only factor in my chronically inflamed body throwing off my hormones and causing my various symptoms and illnesses, but it was a big factor.

Understanding what various foods do to my body (both the good and bad) has taken away the fear I had of my body and health, surprising me with bad news, and has boosted the sparkle, confidence and security I feel in my body. I want you to have the same confidence in your body, health, and be given the information on what some of the things, that may be in your daily diet, could be doing to your beautiful body. Once you know this information, *you* then get to decide if a few changes could boost that sparkle of yours.

I want you to be more in control of your health than you've ever believed possible instead of just worrying or waiting with a "fingers crossed" approach in the hope you don't get ill. You have the power to increase your health and vibrancy to levels you never thought possible. Us women must move away from believing we're bystanders, hoping for good health. We have to realise we can be the creators, and in charge of our own health.

So, let's dig into some of the things that can increase or decrease chronic inflammation and hormonal problems in your body. By even taking on board one or a few of these things, you could immediately start to reduce your inflammation, balance your hormones, and experience other benefits like having better skin, more energy, less PMS and heavy periods.

## Easy Ways To Decrease Inflammation
## And Increase Sparkle

### Wonderful Water

If you were given a beautiful green, flowering plant that was bursting with health and vitality, but you didn't water it, what do you think would happen to it? It'd likely change from being vibrant, healthy, and upright to a sad, lifeless, droopy heap. The same would happen if you just gave it coffee, fizzy drinks and wine, instead of water. Now, not to be rude, but do you ever feel like that plant? Tired, lacklustre, flat, and not like the 'flowering bloom' you once were?

You'll probably put it down to age, being busy, not eating right, your hormones, and yes, all of those things could be adding to your droopiness. However, the reason for women wilting and losing their vibrancy on a daily basis is often because, just like that plant, their body needs some water!

I get it. I, too, want a magic pill to decrease my inflammation, fix my tiredness, balance my hormones, and boost my sparkle. That pill doesn't exist. However, water does.

I haven't yet had a client who hasn't benefited from upping the $H_2O$ in their life. From migraines, exhaustion, low moods, not pooping daily (which btw is crucial for hormonal balance and health), or just wanting the energy to find a partner or new job. The foundation to getting your body to be the best and most sparkly version of itself starts with water. It's what over half your body's composed of.

Water allows every organ in your body to do its job effectively and it's thought even as little as a 2% drop in your optimal hydration levels will make you feel foggy-headed and fatigued. Staying hydrated enables your body to digest food, produce energy, and reduce inflammation. It boosts your metabolism, lubricates your joints, helps get rid of the toxins and waste in your body, and sends electrical messages between your cells so your brain can think, your eyes can see, and your muscles move.

Everyone's water needs are different. However, it's a good idea to drink more water if you drink coffee, tea, alcohol, exercise, or sweat a lot. Start by having at least 1.5-2 litres a day of the best quality* water, or 'sparkle juice' (as I call it). You can either buy a 2 litre glass or stainless steel bottle (plastic contains too many chemicals that mess with your hormones), fill it at the start of each day and try and drink it by about an hour or two before you go to bed.

If you work from home like I do, you can create a 'sparkle juice station' where at the start of each day you fill and cover a 2 litre jug of water and leave it with a glass in an area of your house that you pass through a lot. Every time you see that 'sparkle juice station', you can stop, pour yourself a glass, knowing you're reducing inflammation and helping your body boost your sparkle. If you want to super-boost your sparkle juice, add a pinch of Celtic Sea Salt or Himalayan Salt (not table salt) into your water and you'll be adding precious minerals your body loves and thrives on back into your filtered water (which takes out the crappy stuff from your tap water, but can also take out some of the good minerals too).

Another way to get more water into your cells is to eat foods that contain a high percentage of water like cucumber, spinach, broccoli, tomatoes, apples, and celery. You can add these sorts of fruits and veggies to soups or smoothies too if you'd prefer to not chomp your way through lots of them. You can also make a hydrating 'gel' to drink by adding 2 tablespoons of chia seeds to 2 litres of water. Stir the seeds in the water, cover the jug/vessel and leave it for a few hours (stirring intermittently). This will then turn into a hydrating gel, which you can drink to boost your cells without it feeling like an extra burden on your bladder.

If you're hydrated to a sparkle-boosting level, you'll start to feel more alert, energised, and just generally better. Headaches, fatigue, high or low blood pressure, and even feeling depressed have all eased or disappeared for some people, just through being optimally hydrated. So, it seems that water could be like that magic pill you were looking for after all.

*Make sure you research your local water supplier to find out the chemicals that are added/used as well as the levels of excreted pharmaceuticals like the birth control pill and anti-depressants that are present in your tap water. With this information you can then decide how to obtain the best quality water or water filter that won't disrupt your hormones. This means you're not ingesting unnecessary drugs or chemicals. I personally have invested in a 'Berkey water filter' (well actually I asked for it as a birthday present) as drinking clean water with as few chemicals in as possible is, I believe, one of the best investments we can make for our health.*

## Fabulous Fats

Many of us have grown up with the message that fat is the enemy of good looks and sparkling health. And yes, the pies, pastries, pizzas, and processed foods we all seem to be drawn to are usually full of artificial trans fats (normally listed as 'hydrogenated' or 'partially hydrogenated' oil or fats in the ingredients). These are incredibly inflammatory to our bodies and should be avoided as much as possible.

Also, many cheap, heavily processed seed and vegetable oils (like soybean, corn, rapeseed/canola, sunflower etc) are actually better suited to fueling industrial machinery than our bodies. Some were even classed as "toxic waste" products when they were produced during various manufacturing processes. They're cheap to make and buy but can be costly to our health by increasing inflammation, excess weight, and brain fog. However, let's leave these 'Frankenstein fats' behind and talk about the 'fabulous fats' that we need to eat more of.

Fabulous fats are natural fats that can boost your energy, help balance hormones, and keep you feeling full and satiated for longer. Plus, they enable your beautiful brain to function optimally (your brain is nearly 60% fat, btw).

Start boosting your body by trying to include some minimally processed, fabulous fats in all of your meals or snacks. The best part about these sparkle-boosting fats is that you should start to feel and see the benefits of consuming them quite quickly in your energy, skin, and appetite.

Where you can, add into your daily meals things like avocados, olives, and a variety of nuts and seeds (or nut/seed butters) like brazil, cashew, almond, walnut, chia, hemp, sunflower, pumpkin, and flax. My preferred oils to use in cooking, baking and for dressings are coconut, avocado and extra virgin olive – but, there's also some more unusual oils like hazelnut, walnut and macadamia nut you might like to try. Make sure you look up the 'smoke point' for whichever oil you choose to cook with. This is so you know at what temperature the oil becomes 'unstable' and could release rancid, harmful or inflammatory properties.

Upping your fabulous fats will help create wonderful and healthy forms of energy for your body. They can also help support excess weight loss, improve your memory, regenerate nerve function in your brain, protect against dementia, promote healthy blood flow, plump your skin, and provide a whole host of other sparkle-boosting benefits. So, as much as you can, ditch the 'Frankenstein fats' and get feasting daily on the fabulous ones.

## Gorgeous Greens

When you walk or drive past fields and forests of lush green grasses, trees, or plants, you see vibrancy, life, colour, and beauty. That's because green plants in nature are bursting with health and vitality. Many of the same green plants that keep a variety of animals alive, running around, and thriving in the wild were also given to us to eat because of their inflammation-lowering and health-protective qualities.

So, instead of constantly worrying about the bad (or beige) foods that you need to cut out of your diet, focus instead on adding in vibrantly coloured foods that'll boost your health and sparkle – the main colour I'd  love you to increase is gorgeous (leafy) greens. If you want an instant body-boost, then start with gorgeous greens in every meal, every day if possible – it's what I make all my clients do as much as they're able and they see great results. This is because gorgeous greens can boost your energy and immune system, and help your liver function at its best (which you want in tip-top condition if you want to get rid of excess hormones, excess weight, and other toxins that can make you feel crappy and tired).

Try a veggie-based green smoothie with your breakfast. There are lots of 'green smoothie' recipes out there so find one you like or create one yourself using spinach, nut butter, non-dairy milk, and some fruit. Add a handful of rocket or watercress to your lunch. Add some cabbage, brussels, kale, bok choi or broccoli to your dinner and voila, your body will automatically be boosted by those gorgeous greens.

Something I do (which always gets strange looks from my husband), I'll often take a handful of rocket, lettuce, or spinach, roll it into a ball in my hands and then "down it in one" for a big, quick hit of greens. I call this a 'rocket shot' and do it if I've not managed to get any greens into my meals so far that day. I can down strong-tasting greens like I used to down strong tasting alcohol – the great news for my body is, the former decreases my inflammation, whereas the latter increased it.

So, why not get guzzling those gorgeous greens and you too could start to have the same spring in your step as a bunny that's been munching on grass and leaves all day long.

## Extractor Fan Eating

I know organic produce is more expensive, but if you can even buy just a few organic items, then do (or you could try and grow a few things of your own quite easily and cheaply – even in window boxes). Some studies have come out claiming there's no nutritional difference between organic and non-organic food. However, it's not the nutritional value we're disputing of non-organic food. It's the hormones and antibiotics that can be routinely used in factory-farmed meat (especially pork) and dairy production and the chemical pesticides sprayed onto your fruit and veg (with some of these now actually proven to be cancer-causing substances as well as disrupting your hormones).

At the very least, wash all of your fruits and veggies thoroughly before eating them to remove as much of the pesticides/chemical residue on them as you can. Also, look at frozen organic fruit and veg because this can sometimes be a more cost-effective way of buying it.

Stay updated on the items that've been shown to consistently contain high levels of pesticides, antibiotics, and hormones (these often change every few years and will vary depending on the country you live in, as each country has different farming practices). Simply do an internet search for 'Clean Fifteen' and 'Dirty Dozen' fruits and vegetables in the country you live in. This should tell you which ones are better bought organic as they absorb the most chemicals/pesticides or, the ones that don't need to be because they generally contain or absorb fewer chemicals/pesticides.

A crucial thing to remember is that it's still more important for your health and sparkle to eat a wide variety of fruits and veggies every day instead of avoiding them simply because you can't buy organic and are worried about the potential chemicals found on/in them. Fruits and veggies have huge inflammation fighting properties (antioxidants). One of the best things you can do for your health (especially if it's seriously struggling) is to aim to have at least 2-3 portions of fruit and 5-7 portions of veggies each day if you can. If not every day, then aim for 3 times a week to start with. I know that sounds like a lot, but a morning smoothie (I try and add some berries, pineapple, banana, a handful of spinach and a chunk of raw courgette – which makes the smoothie creamy – random, but true), a side salad with your lunch (like some rocket, peppers and beetroot) and some veggies with your dinner (like broccoli and carrots) and boom! That's 3 portions of fruit of 7 of veggies to help lower your risk of some super nasty diseases and boost your health, hormones and sparkle.

Eating more fruits and veggies (along with the other things we've talked about so far) can help change the 'environment' of your body. This is so needed if we want to not just improve upon short-term, specific diseases, or symptoms, but help prevent as many as possible in the long-term. The modern way of looking at and treating disease is often to focus in on the area/condition/disease and spot treat it. This is fine and often needed, but we must then look at the environment of the body and why it wasn't able to get rid of or fight off the disease/condition/symptom that it's generally designed to be able to do.

I like to think of it as having an area of mould in your bathroom i.e. the disease/condition/symptom. Now, we don't want to leave the mould there so it gets worse, so we can buy an anti-mould spray (i.e. medication/an operation/supplements/other treatments etc). However, if we don't install an extractor fan in the bathroom, the mould will usually come back. It may come back in the same or a different area because the environment that enabled it to form/grow hasn't been changed. The short-term focus and immediate solutions can be on getting rid of the mould, yet the long-term solution and focus must be on installing an extractor fan.

For instance, having my breast tumour removed (the mould) was the right thing for me to do. But, to carry on with the same stressful life and bad dietary habits I had would've meant I was increasing my chances for the 'mould' to come back. I was permanently terrified for the first 6 months after my operations of the 'mould' returning and it not getting spotted or treated before it spread. However, learning about all the things I could do to reduce inflammation in my body, like eat lots more fruits and veggies, and making various lifestyle changes has been like bringing in the best extractor fan to my body. It doesn't mean there won't ever be any mould again. It just means I've lessened the chances and done all I can to change the environment that produced it so I don't have to live in fear.

# Limit These To Decrease Inflammation And Increase Your Sparkle

## Stress and Sugar

When our bodies are chronically inflamed, hormones imbalanced, and energy is low, we can feel old before our time – this can make us feel thoroughly sparkle-less. Scientifically speaking, 'ageing' is your body's tissue deteriorating due to cellular inflammation. This inflammation speeds up the aging process, sends your hormones haywire, decreases your energy, and can trigger various diseases. The biggest causes of inflammation I see for women right now are largely caused by two sparkle stealing baddies – stress and high blood sugar.

i)     **Stress**

Your body is designed to (in most instances) be able to heal itself if it's given the right conditions, and inflammation actually helps with that. Inflammation is there to help fight off anything that'll make you unwell – so remember, it's super handy when you cut yourself or get an infection. The problem, as we've been talking about, comes when inflammation becomes chronic due to constant stress and stressors (from our thoughts, diet, and environment). And too many women are suffering from various conditions and diseases caused by this chronic inflammation.

I'm guessing you think your constant high stress levels are just the way things are and have to be in this modern world? You may think that unless you win the lottery, your kids get a full-time nanny, your parents don't get ill and your mortgage gets paid off, then there's no way you can reduce your stress levels.

I'm going to get real with you now because your health, happiness, and sparkle depends on you not thinking daily, hourly stress is as normal to a woman's life as breathing. I don't want you to keep ignoring your body's stressed-out signals – consistent low energy, headaches, painful periods, bad skin, gut issues and worse – and live your life running on adrenaline and coffee. It's far too dangerous!

Short-term stress and inflammation, can help us run from danger, act quickly and send help and healing to parts of our body. Constant stress and inflammation though has serious side-effects – it robs you of energy, imbalances your hormones, decreases your fertility, prematurely ages your skin, can cause acne, hair loss or hair thinning, decreases your sex drive, lowers your immunity, and makes you susceptible to a whole host of other diseases and negative consequences.

Did you know that when a person is receiving an organ transplant, to ensure that their immune system doesn't kick into full gear and reject the 'foreign' organ, they're given stress hormones to suppress their immune system? The effect of stress hormones in your body is THAT powerful. Your immune system is there to protect you from everything from an infected cut, common cold and cough, to cancer. You don't want to be minimising its power or signalling for it to be shut off or reduced by stress hormones because you refuse to ask for help or look at even the smallest ways to reduce your stress levels.

If you're serious about getting your sparkle back, balancing your hormones, having enough energy, feeling and looking better, then it's time to de-stress and simplify your life. Even in just one or two small areas. Get used to telling people who make constant demands of you 'no, no, no' instead of just telling your body to 'go, go, go'. Start working with your hormonal cycle because working against it (and living like a man) is very stressful to your beautiful female body. Consider reducing or stopping watching stressful media reports or TV shows that make you tense, fearful, upset, or play on your mind. You can even speak to a professional who can talk to you about the things you don't want to talk to friends or family about. Ask for more help from those around you with day to day tasks and stop struggling on your own (read more about this in the 'Speak-up For Your Sparkle' chapter).

Take time to pray, meditate, or if that's not your thing, just have 5 minutes of breathing deeply every day when you're sat on the toilet, if you have no other free time. Read books that can help teach you how to reduce stress in certain areas of your life or uplift you. Listen to music that calms you or makes you feel super happy. Diffuse essential oils that are known to help calm your body and mind (my favourite is frankincense) and reduce the amount of time you spend with people who cause your stress levels to soar.

When you feel extra stressed or have experienced a particularly stressful time or episode where your body is feeling anxious, jittery, and horrible, you can help your energy and health with a 'cortisol flush'. This is to quickly help move stress hormones out of your body so your immune system isn't seriously impaired, and reduce any other harm that circulating stress hormones can cause your body.

A cortisol flush is similar to what animals do after a stressful episode e.g. if a gazelle is gently grazing and then is chased by a lion who wants to kill her, her whole body will be filled with the stress hormones of adrenaline and cortisol as she runs for her life. If she outruns the lion, she doesn't spend hours, days, weeks, years holding onto that stress and fear so it increases her chances of disease in her body. Generally, most animals like the gazelle engage in some sort of vigorous body shake or movement to move the adrenaline and cortisol out of their body. This enables them to resume peaceful grazing or relaxing within a short space of time of literally running for their lives and therefore, protects their long-term health from this short-term panic and stress.

This is a tool I want you to use. If you've experienced a shock or feel like your body is filled with stress from being too busy/angry/something else, you can either do some vigorous movement like 5 minutes on a rebounder trampoline (these are an excellent way to increase your circulation and health), some wild dancing (better if no one else is around), or a short run (even on the spot) will all help your body come back into balance. Or, if you feel you don't have any energy or inclination for this sort of short and intense movement then you can have an orgasm (alone or with a partner) because this will achieve the same effect in your body (although maybe don't do this one if you're at work in an office). Both these things will help flush the stress hormones from your body and bring you back into a state of balance to prevent further mental and physical depletion or increase your risk of hormonal imbalance or unwanted symptoms/diseases.

Once a month, take a few moments to check in with yourself and write down the things causing your body and mind the greatest amount of stress and anxiety. A good time to do this is during your period or when there's a new moon. The new moon is when the moon is totally hidden and a woman on her period tends to want to retreat and be hidden too, so women can feel naturally reflective and get great insights at these times. So, is it your finances, job, children, or a general feeling of overwhelm that you can't explain? Look for the smallest of ways to begin easing some of these issues that are keeping you consistently stressed, including asking others for help – which many women are terrible at. You were always meant to exist in a tribe. You were always meant to be able to ask a neighbour, friend, or family member to literally or metaphorically "hold the baby" if you need a break or help.

One month when I was reflecting on why I was feeling particularly stressed, I realised it was because on top of a busy period at work, I had lots of my friends' children to shop for with upcoming birthdays. I felt really overwhelmed trying to think of presents, buy them, wrap them, and send them whilst trying to run my business. So, because I'd identified this as an unnecessary stressor in my life, I just stopped buying and sending presents to my friends' kids. That one action (that has lost me no friends btw) has stopped stress in an area that used to consistently panic and stress me out.

Another month, I was getting overwhelmed with the housework and feeling like I was never able to get on top of it. I spoke (ok, moaned) to a friend and she told me to check out 'The Organised Mum Method'. Oh my goodness, this revolutionary process (headed up by the gorgeous Gemma

Bray) has eased so much stress in this area of my life (and hundreds of thousands of other women's too). Go check out her website www.theorganisedmum.blog, buy her book *The Organised Mum Method* (btw, you don't have to be a mum for this to be helpful) or download 'The Team TOMM' app if you, like me, get easily stressed out in trying to run a home and doing all the other day to day things in your life.

What about you? What's one thing that someone else might find super easy to do but you, for whatever reason, gets stressed out by it? How could you change that situation to reduce inflammation in your body and protect your health and sparkle? You weren't created to live with constant, unrelenting stress, so stop ignoring and normalising it and start reducing it. If you get serious about this one area, I believe it can have *the* most radical effect on boosting your health and sparkle. As your stress levels go down, your sparkle will automatically go up.

ii)     **Sugar**

Stress and sugar are often partners in crime. The more stress we have in our lives (which usually exhausts or upsets us), usually the more sugar we want or eat to try and claw back some energy and comfort. So, if you can reduce your stress, even just a little, then your need to always eat things that are full of sugar will usually decrease.

There's no two ways about it. Refined sugar is one of the biggest sparkle stealers out there for women. I'm not talking about the sugar in fruit or vegetables because these also contain fibre and a whole host of other health-protecting and boosting properties. I'm talking about the refined sugar that's added to foods (often without you realising) and is found in biscuits, sweets, cakes, breads, pastry, and other highly-processed foods. Often some of the things you want more of as a woman – better skin, less diseases, and more energy can be found by simply cutting back on or breaking up with sugar.

We all know the good feelings that sugar can bring. However, many of us don't know about the not so sweet side of this common ingredient. Sugar is a bit of a sneaky thief, and while it seems to be "gifting" you with immediate energy, it then does a clever 'bag swap' and leaves you with more inflammation and less energy, health, and sparkle than you had before.

Women gravitate towards sugar because it gives them that energy hit that's so often needed. In reality, it's not actually the best form of energy for you because it'll spike and then crash your energy, leaving you feeling more tired.

Think of sugar like this. It's like a cheating boyfriend who may seem sexy and attractive but always loves and leaves you with lower energy and moods than you had before (and possibly some nasty diseases too in the long-term). This is because constantly eating things with refined sugar will mean there's excess glucose in your blood stream which causes inflammation. This can then result in all sorts of unwanted diseases, hormonal problems, damage to your skin and makes you always crave more. Possibly not so sweet after all, is it?

Recently, my husband was embarking on going sugar free to lose some excess weight and I said I'd support him and completely give up refined sugar with him for two weeks. Wow, I was pretty shocked at how hard the sugar withdrawal hit us both. We suffered from two days of feeling depressed, having headaches, low energy, and feeling "obsessed" with thinking about sugary foods. However, once we got past this withdrawal stage, we actually felt the opposite – lighter, brighter, and excess weight that had crept up over winter, just fell off easily.

Reducing refined sugar in my diet was one of the hardest things for me to do when I found out how badly it was affecting my female body. But, it was also one of the most crucial things that helped me get rid of my adult acne, PCOS, balance my hormones, and reduce the other inflammatory conditions that were plaguing my whole life. I now try and limit the amount of refined sugar I have but, I do allow myself some really intentional moments of sugary pleasure. You can find out how I manage to do that whilst also keeping my inflammation down at the same time, in the 'Sexy Sparkle' chapter.

As well as reading the 'Sexy Sparkle' chapter in this book I'd encourage you to read *'The End of Overeating'* by Dr David A. Kessler to find out how and why so many of us have become hooked on refined sugar. It's a fascinating read and a must for anyone who would describe themselves as a "sugar addict". It'll also show you all the ways it's hidden from you like it being called about 60 different names that you wouldn't recognise as "sugar" so you *don't* realise its sugar on an ingredients list.

I'm not saying don't ever have a pleasure-filled, sugary treat. What's most important is to know that if you're feeling exhausted or unwell mentally or physically, a diet that has a lot of refined sugar in it will exponentially increase the inflammation in your body, and almost definitely make you feel worse. Just start looking for some simple and small ways to reduce your sugar intake. Swap juice and fizzy drinks for water. Check food labels to make sure sugar hasn't been snuck in where it's not needed. Cook more of your own meals from scratch. Don't add sugar into tea and coffee. Find some non-sugary snacks like nuts or nut butter with fruit that you really enjoy, and increase fabulous fats and gorgeous greens in your diet. This will help you feel fuller, have more energy, keep your blood sugar steady, your hormones balanced, and help you sparkle more throughout the day.

*NB. If you've been diagnosed with a serious illness or are suffering from a chronic inflammatory condition, then I always suggest that sugar be one of the first things to remove from your diet because it can help to reduce inflammation and give your body a better chance of being able to fight illness/disease.*

## Dodgy Drinks For Dames

Part of having a truly sparkle-filled life is indulging in moments and times of pleasure (you'll found out why this is vital for your health, later on in the book). I'm a big advocate of you living your best, not boring life. However, there are two drinks many women love that generally don't love them back in the same way. I'm not going to tell you that you can't ever have them – remember that's for *you* to decide once you have all the information – I'm simply going to tell you how they might be affecting your health, hormones, and sparkle.

## Alcohol

Now, I'm no party pooper. I know a glass of bubbles or other tipple is a great way to celebrate, socialise, or just unwind after a stressful day. However, after a decade of partying and hard drinking (and I mean hard!), I wasn't surprised to find out that alcohol's a bit of a baddie for women's bodies. In fact, I'm downplaying it because in fact it's downright toxic to our bodies. You're an adult, so I'm not going to beat around the bush or sugar coat this info. I'm just going to give you the cold hard facts about what it can do to your body and sparkle, and then you can decide how much you do or don't have it in your life.

First and foremost, alcohol is super inflammatory to your female body (I'm hoping by now you understand that if you don't want heavy periods, PMS, skin and gut issues or other diseases, then you don't want to constantly be having things that increase inflammation in your body). Alcohol dehydrates and damages your skin, prevents you from getting the health-boosting deep sleep that your body needs, can make depression and anxiety worse, interferes with your hormones and so, if you're experiencing any sort of hormonal issues alcohol will likely make it worse. It's classed as a Group 1 carcinogen (the same as tobacco and asbestos) that increases a woman's risk of breast cancer.

I'm not telling you this to scare you or stop you drinking completely, I just think it's your right as a woman to know this stuff before you get giddy about 'Gin'O'Clock' or 'Prosecco Time'. I didn't know this stuff. I had to find it out for myself when I wanted to prevent getting another breast tumour. And to be honest, I'm a bit pissed about not being told about the health consequences of consistently getting pissed (or just regularly drinking). I thought alcohol's only negative trait was that it gave me hangovers – and they seemed a good trade-off for all the fun and socialising drinking brought me. However, the trade-off was actually that my long-term health was being compromised for short-term fun. No one told me that the thing many women use to unwind or treat themselves after a hard day can be directly linked to so many "women's problems" i.e. hormonal issues that can cause a lot of serious pain and suffering to women.

Drinking alcohol every day increases circulating oestrogen levels in your body, and as I touched on earlier, this excess of oestrogen can cause everything from bad skin, raging PMS, painful periods, PCOS, to more serious things like certain cancers. Alcohol is actually broken down in your body into a cancer-causing chemical that's called acetaldehyde. This is 30 times more toxic than alcohol to your body, damages your DNA, and can prevent your body from being able to repair this damage. This is why the after-effects of drinking can make us feel so terrible as our body tries to get rid of these dangerous toxins. Your liver prioritises trying to get rid of the toxins from alcohol, meaning it has less capacity to process and get rid of excess oestrogen or stress hormones that can imbalance your hormones and cause you a variety of problems.

Since I learned this information, I hardly ever drink alcohol as it affects my sparkle far too much. When I first found out the information I've shared with you, I stopped drinking alcohol completely for 10 years as I was so fearful of its links to breast cancer. I now maybe have an alcoholic drink 2 or 3 times a year for celebrations but, I make sure I do all I can to offset it's toxins by not drinking excessively, drinking extra water, making sure I'm relaxed and happy and not stressed, and eating foods that help my liver process alcohol like gorgeous green leafy veg.

You must make the decision that's right for you and your health with the information and health goals you have. If I have a client who's seriously ill or struggling with a health issue, then I always advise that alcohol is dramatically reduced or cut out to lower their body's 'toxic load' and inflammation. But, again, this has to be their choice. The idea or experience of having a lighter, pain-free, less-exhausting period or clear skin, has to make them happier than that daily glass of wine.

If you do decide that reducing or cutting out alcohol is something that's right for you, then know you're not stuck with just having tumblers of fruit juice. There are now some *really* good low or no-alcohol drinks out there (I'm currently drinking a 'Clean Gin' and tonic as I write this). I still absolutely adore the ritual and feeling of a cold drink of bubbles from a champagne flute. However, I now want it without the crappy effects that alcoholic fizz has on my body. So, one of my favourite sparkly drinks of choice is kombucha*. This 2,000-year-old drink was used by ancient Chinese communities to boost their health and energy. They even called it the 'Immortal Health Elixir' due to its health-benefits. Authentic kombucha has an unusual taste that can take some time getting used to. It's tangy and tastes mildly alcoholic. I love it because it feels like an 'adult' drink, instead of other soft drinks that can make me feel like I'm having a sugar-laden kids' drink. Whether you trade this for some of your alcoholic drinks or not, I'd still encourage you to add it into your diet. Here's just a few of kombucha's sparkle-boosting benefits:

- It's rich in antioxidants and these can boost your immune system and energy levels.
- It's packed with probiotics which can boost your gut's good bacteria (which in turn can also boosts your immune system and overall health).
- It's anti-inflammatory (and we *always* want to be reducing that pesky inflammation in our bodies to be super sparkly).
- It can help reduce the risk of infections (due to its ability to help boost your immune system).

- It's considered a cancer preventative by some because it's rich in many of the bacterial acids and enzymes that your body uses for detoxification.
- It can improve digestion.
- It can help fight candida/yeast overgrowth.
- It can help with arthritic joints as it contains glucosamine, which is a treatment and prevention for arthritis.

*\* Some of my favourite kombucha companies can be found at the back of this book in the 'Sparkly Recommendations' section.*

## Coffee

I know, I know. I've told you things about alcohol you probably didn't want to know and now I'm messing with your coffee. But, I have to tell you that drinking excess coffee (or other caffeinated drinks) is generally not something that'll help you feel consistently wonderful as a woman. Will treating yourself to a great quality coffee once a day or a few times a week ruin your health? Of course not. Will drinking it from the moment you wake up to keep you going throughout the day be the best thing for your health, hormones, and sparkle? I'm afraid not.

Why? Well, the caffeine in coffee, especially when consumed first thing in the morning without any kind of food, messes with your hormones by causing your body to produce extra stress hormones. This increases inflammation, which can interfere with ovulation and deplete your energy, libido, overall health, and leave you with brain fog and fatigue – the opposite of feeling sparkly. It can also increase the propensity of your breasts or ovaries to produce cysts. Lots of conventionally grown coffee also contains mold, pesticides, and other toxins which you don't want to be drip-feeding into your beautiful body all day long because that can affect your energy and health.

If you can, save coffee (and its ensuing hormone havoc) as a pleasure-filled ritual and treat. Try not to have more than one or a maximum of two cups a day and always have it with some sort of food, before about 2pm. This is so it doesn't interfere with your sleep because on average it can take your body about 5-6 hours to eliminate half the caffeine from your body (btw caffeine and alcohol take longer to leave women's bodies than men's so we can suffer from more of the negative effects as we have them in our systems longer).

Some people do better with coffee and caffeine in general than others, and this is to do with the fact that some people can break down and eliminate caffeine from their body more quickly than others (this is genetic). Take your cues from your body. If you're feeling terrible, suffering from exhaustion, anxiety, hormonal imbalances, and drink coffee all day, then try a different routine for a while and see if it makes a difference.

Consider always starting your day with a glass of water first thing to boost your hydration too.

I personally don't recommend decaf coffee as an alternative to coffee due to the chemicals that are often used in the process of removing caffeine, and the fact that the green beans used can sometimes contain some of the highest levels of mold, pesticides, and other toxins which can cause inflammation. I think if you want a coffee then don't settle for an unnaturally modified version of it. Have the best quality coffee, in its most natural state, and enjoy every mouthful. If your body is unable to tolerate that, then maybe take that as a clear message from your body that for you it's not a good match and it's time to date some other drinks.

Teas such as green, black, and white tea also contains caffeine. However, once brewed, they contain less than coffee. So, I'd suggest the same advice if tea is your caffeinated go-to, of sticking to no more than 1-2 mugs before 2pm. I love my daily green tea and when I need or want the energy-boosting effects of caffeine from a drink, but also want to make sure I get other big health-benefits, I have an organic matcha green tea. This is my sparkly morning ritual a few times a week because this tea (loved by Japanese monks) gives you an alert, but not 'wired' feeling that gently tapers off, as opposed to crashes out. It has high levels of the lovely L-theanine, a calming amino acid, which affects your brain in a similar way to meditation and reduces your heart rate in response to stress. Although just like coffee, you don't want to have it on an empty stomach or drink more than one cup a day, if you're wanting to balance your hormones. I always blend my matcha with some coconut butter (so the fat helps lessen the 'hit' of caffeine on my body) and add some organic vanilla essence to create a creamy, naturally sweet and comforting drink.

Here's just a few of the other reason's I love matcha since it was recommended to me by a nutritionist after my breast tumour operations:

- It can increase your energy.
- It naturally contains high levels of EGCG which is anti-inflammatory and been shown to have some powerful anti-cancer properties.
- It can boost your concentration and memory.
- It can help strengthen your immune system.
- It can help detoxify your body.
- It can help calm your mind.
- It is thought to have greater antioxidant potency (which helps to bring inflammation down) than broccoli, blueberries, pomegranate, goji berries, and dark chocolate combined!

If you're trying to get or are currently pregnant then I suggest staying away from all caffeine and sticking to herbal or fruit teas. If you don't like these and want something that has an earthier, more roasted flavor then Kukicha (a twig tea) with some cashew milk, can hit the spot.

So, why not have some fun and experiment with different drinks? Maybe you'll find some alternatives to alcohol and coffee that you love just as much and don't increase inflammation in your body and throw off your hormones. Remember, if you are going to have these drinks, then try to choose great quality versions, have them with food, take a little longer to drink them, drink them less often if possible and then, enjoy every single sip as opposed to downing them when you're stressed (which would cause a double inflammation hit to your body).

## Ditch Or Decrease Dairy

Don't think I can't hear your cries of, "Noooo, I can't give up cheese!" because I said the same after being told it'd be best for my hormonal health to ditch dairy. Food is powerful stuff and if our health and sparkle isn't where we want it to be, then we must look at why. Food and drinks contain vital information that 'speak' to your cells and determine a large portion of your health, energy, and vitality every, single, day (along with your thoughts, feelings, and environment).

Your mental and physical health is something you have the power and ability to boost or reduce with every bite or sip you take, which is pretty amazing. Stick with taking in this info a little longer, even if we're discussing some of your favourite things, because I know you can handle the truth. Like they say, "The truth will set you free" – and in this case, hopefully set you free from feeling crappy and struggling with low moods, bad skin, painful periods, excess weight or whatever's stopping your sparkle right now.

So, let's discuss dairy. If your aim is to get your sparkle back and stay in your best mental and physical health, then I'd really recommend you look to totally ditch or massively decrease dairy in your diet. It's helped me and so many of my clients stop suffering from skin or period issues that'd plagued us for years.

I found out just how dodgy it can be for a woman's body during my research to cut out any foods that would inflame my body, imbalance my hormones, or put me at a higher risk of developing a breast tumour again. This led me to pretty much ditch dairy from my diet. The reason dairy is such a sparkle-stealer is because it's from lactating mummy cows whose milk is loaded with oestrogen for their young. Oestrogen has a growth-stimulating effect – which you want if you're a baby cow, but not if you've got a tumour like I had or are struggling with your weight. Excess oestrogen in your body can trigger or worsen PMS, painful periods, skin, or hormonal issues – all of which too many women are struggling with.

Cow's milk should really be labelled as 'baby cow growth juice' if we're to understand its true purpose as 'fattening fuel' for little calves – not something for us to have throughout our days. It contains natural and (often in industrialised dairy production) artificial hormones to stimulate milk production in the mummy cow, and help turn a baby calf into a great big, cow. It's designed perfectly for the growth of that baby cow, in just the same way human milk is perfectly designed to help a baby grow into a healthy, strong child.

Cow's milk contains the protein A1 casein, which human bodies can't properly digest (because we're not cows). This produces an inflammatory response in your gut (regardless of whether you think you're okay with milk or not). If you're eating and drinking dairy most days with most meals and snacks, then you're increasing inflammation in your body, which can create the perfect environment to trigger or exacerbate hormonal imbalances and other negative health issues.

Before you decide that "life's too short" and dairy in your daily diet is something you simply can't give up (believe me, I used to feel exactly the same), do your own research and look at what's legally allowed to end up in your family's milk, cream, and cheese (if you're not a fan of poo and puss, then it's not great news). Also, I'd urge you to look into what a cow has to go through to produce milk for humans instead of her calves. I've only recently found this out (as my reasons previously were always about my health as opposed to the animals) – it's actually heart-breaking.

A cow's pregnancy is about 9 months long – the same as a human. In order for humans to be able to drink the milk that a cow has produced for her baby, a baby cow has to be removed from its mother at around one day old. The mother cow is known to cry for days due to her baby being taken away. This information made me so upset and feel selfish (as well as angry that I hadn't been told this before). I love animals and don't want any cow carrying its baby for nine months, going through the process of giving birth only to have it cruelly taken away just so I can have its milk in my tea.

Some seriously incredible non-dairy milks, yoghurts, cheeses, and chocolates are now being produced (although always check the labels to make sure you pick ones with natural not ultra-processed ingredients). You can find the ones I absolutely love and recommend to my clients in the 'Sparkly Recommendations' section. So, why not try a few of them because I believe you'll reap the benefits of not having inflammatory 'baby cow growth juice' as a staple in your sparkly diet. Our power as women is in being informed and not ignorant of where our food comes, how it's produced, and the effect it has on our bodies and our world.

Very occasionally I'll still eat some dairy. For example, if I'm eating at someone else's house, I don't like them getting stressed about what can feel like a lot of dietary requirements from me. I just tell them that I don't eat meat and happily eat whatever else they serve me. This keeps mine and their stress levels low, and keeping my stress low has a bigger positive effect on my overall health than me making sure every little thing I try and not eat daily is never put on my plate.

I've not told you any of this information because I want you to do exactly as I've done. And I don't want you panicked that you have to make lots of big, permanent changes immediately – as that can be super stressful. Every step on the path back to your sparkle has to be what's right for you and there may be some trial and error involved. However, if you have health concerns, especially hormonal ones, I want you to have the information my clients have, which I also wish I'd been given years ago when I felt so sad and helpless with my health struggles.

## Crazy Chemicals

Every day, possibly without even knowing it, you're stressing your beautiful body and harming your hormones and health by using crazy amounts of chemicals that your body just wasn't deigned to process. It's been said that we're exposed to more chemicals in a month (through our air, cars, homes, work, food, water, and personal products) than our grandparents were exposed to in a lifetime. It's thought most women leave the house each day with at least 300 chemicals on their body after they've got ready for the day (think of the chemical cocktail from shower gels, shampoos, make-up, perfumes etc). Whether those figures are exact or not, the truth is we're facing an unprecedented overload of toxic substances that our bodies weren't designed to absorb, inhale, or consume. These chemicals can give us everything from brain fog and low energy to much more serious health conditions. Many of the chemicals in our favourite personal or cleaning products are known as 'endorcine-disriptors' – that basically means they mess up your hormones. Another fancy word for lots of them are xeno-oestrogens – that means that when they're in your body they mimic oestrogen so increase the oestrogen dominance that causes so many of the hormonal problems women struggle with.

On a day-to-day basis, we have limited control over global issues concerning traffic, air, or water pollution (apart from investing in good water filters and also telling our governments that we want action taken to stop big companies polluting our world). However, we *can* control what goes in and onto our bodies to give them the best chance of staying super sparkly. It's been proven that certain chemicals sprayed on our food or used in household or beauty products can cause everything from hormone imbalances, skin problems, breathing issues, to cancer. So, let's start being more mindful and clearing out some of these crazy chemicals from our daily lives. Our bodies are pretty clever at getting rid of toxic waste from our systems but let's help them out by not unnecessarily overloading them. We don't want our bodies having to spend more time neutralising harmful chemicals from our kitchen cleaning spray, than making energy or repairing damaged or diseased cells.

Here's some of the biggest areas that I make my clients look at and begin to change when they want to super-boost their sparkle, balance their hormones, and optimise their health and energy. You don't need to change all of your products in one fell swoop (unless you're seriously ill or have the gusto and finances to). Start with one or two of the things you use every day and look for more natural, organic, less toxic alternatives every time you need to replace an item.

**Beauty And Body Care** – *This includes make-up, body lotion, toothpaste, hand-soap, shower gel, shampoo, conditioner, perfume, sanitary towels, and tampons.*

Start looking for products with the least amount of chemicals, ingredients, and the most organic/natural brands. Overall, just try and reduce the number of actual products you use on your skin. I'm not asking you to turn into a no-product stinker. I adore my make-up and lotions and potions, but things like swapping your chemical-laden body lotion for coconut oil or changing from having a separate face wash, shower gel, and hand soap to something versatile like *Dr. Bronner's castile soap* will make a huge difference to your daily chemical consumption. Also, look to change your sanitary products to organic ones because most of what you're putting in/near that highly absorbable and sensitive area contains a lot of toxic chemicals. Ever wondered why there's no information on your sanitary products about the chemicals in them? It's because they don't want you to know and legally don't have to tell you (oh and the big companies that own the biggest brands of feminine hygiene products, and make billions from creating these chemical-laden pads and tampons, are all currently run by men in case you're interested!) You'll find my fave organic and sustainable options in the 'Sparkly Recommendations' section – including www.wearemout.co.uk pads – a female run brand doing amazing things to change the conversation around periods, period products and reduce the chemicals put in women's bodies and the impact disposable products have on our environment.

Deodorant is another biggie for women. Many anti-perspirants use aluminum salts to block your sweat glands and there's a possible link between this and breast cancer. I for one no longer take the risk with my health by blocking up an important detox area of my body with cheap anti-perspirants and I'd love you not to, either.

Consider choosing a natural deodorant because there's now some really good ones out there. It may take some testing on your part to find one that works for you and your lifestyle but please persevere. This is something that generally goes on and into your body every day, so I'd always suggest prioritising this to research and buy (again, my personal recommendations are at the back of this book).

Here's a quick list of some of the nastiest chemicals that you don't want in your beauty products or being put on your loved ones. Take a look at the labels of the products you're using every day and see if they contain any of these nasties:

- **Sodium Lauryl Sulfate (SLS) / Sodium Laureth Sulfate (SLES).** These chemicals make products foam and are known to cause skin, lung, and eye irritation. You'll find them in over 90% of cleaning and body/hair products. The biggest worry is that when they mix with other chemicals they can form cancer-causing substances (carcinogens), so you want to avoid or minimise the amount of stuff you use with these in.

- **Parabens.** These are preservatives that stop yeast, mold, and bacteria from growing in your cosmetics. They have properties that mimic oestrogen and have been found in biopsies of breast tumours. You want to try and avoid anything that contains something with a word that ends in paraben: Methylparaben, Ethylparaben, Propylparaben, Butylparaben, Isobutylparaben, Isopropylparaben etc. Sometimes companies (so you can't spot those pesky parabens that more people are trying to avoid) will abbreviate the above ingredients as 'ethyl', 'butyl', 'methy' and 'propyl' etc. How dishonest and dodgy does that feel in terms of keeping vital information from us?

- **Triclosan.** This is a known hormone disruptor and especially interferes with your skin, reproductive hormones, and thyroid.

- **Fragrance.** Now this a shadowy, general term and means you don't know what you're putting on your precious skin and therefore in your or your loved ones' body. This vague labelling is meant to protect companies from people stealing their formulas. However, when mixes of fragrances have been associated with skin, breathing, and reproductive issues, surely we have the right to know what we're putting on our skin and into our bodies.

- **Phthalates.** These are known to cause hormone disruption and have been linked with everything from early breast development in girls to an increased risk of breast cancer and birth defects in the reproductive organs of both males and females.

- **Sunscreen chemicals.** These chemicals, found in non-organic or non-natural sunscreens, are disruptive to your hormones and have been linked with cancers and cell damage. Some of the names used for them are avobenzone, oxybenzone (which also goes by benzophenone-3), octinoxate (which can also be shown as octyl methoxycinnamate, methoxy-cinnamate, ethylhexyl methoxy-cinnamate, or simply OMC), homosalate and PABA. So, don't boost your health with the sunshine, only to ruin it with your sunscreen.

- **Formaldehyde.** This chemical is meant to prolong the life of your products by stopping the growth of bacteria. However, it's been classified as a carcinogen to humans and is also known to cause skin allergies and damage the immune system.

- **Synthetic colours.** These come from tar and petroleum sources, and are thought to be a human carcinogen and skin irritant. Your food and cosmetic product labels will contain letters, a colour, and number to show synthetic colours are present. Try and avoid them as much as you can.

**Household** – *This includes synthetic air fresheners, scented candles, bleach, laundry powder/liquid, fabric softener, dishwasher tablets, rinse aid, and cleaning products.*

Try and protect your home, which is your sparkle sanctuary, from crazy amounts of chemicals. Get rid of them or look to change to a more natural version with fewer/no chemicals. Many chemicals found in these products are toxic and what's called 'bio-accumulative'. This means once they get into your system, they stay there (they don't get excreted) and so can increase your risk of autoimmune diseases and cancer as they accumulate.

Look for non-toxic, plant-based cleaning products (although be careful of something called 'green-washing' where companies use packaging and wording that make you think they're not toxic but actually they still contain lots of chemicals). There are countless blogs/websites about the ways to create a less toxic household and many even teach you how you can make your own cleaning products cheaply with things like lemon, baking soda, vinegar, and essential oils. The ThinkDirty app is brilliant and can show you how good or toxic your beauty or household products are so you can make some switches.

Reducing the toxic load your body has to carry can make a huge difference not only to your health but that of your family and pets as well.

The last thing to say about the information from this whole section of the book is please don't get stressed, panicky, and paranoid about all of these crazy chemicals or health-dampening effects of the certain foods and drinks I've listed. If, for whatever reason, you can't make any changes right now, then that's fine. Because constant stress, worry and paranoia over food or living without chemicals and things that disrupt your hormones can be just as (and I'd even go so far as to say more) unhealthy for you. I suffered for a while from something called 'orthorexia' – which is when people become so obsessed with not eating anything 'bad' for them, they can't live or socialise in a normal way.

After my breast tumour, I was so scared of eating or drinking anything that caused inflammation, imbalanced my hormones, or increased my risk of breast cancer that I panicked at or avoided certain social situations if I couldn't control there being anything organic or what I deemed as 'healthy'. Thank goodness I realised that this chronic stress was far more dangerous and inflammatory to my body than enjoying a piece of birthday cake with friends or having a happy family meal that contained non-organic carrots.

Your body is incredible and works every moment of every day to do all it can to keep you in health – as it's designed to do. However, it just needs a helping hand from you so that it can do its joyful job of keeping you in balance even better. So, be empowered. Know about what certain foods/products do to your precious body with regard to inflammation and your hormones. Then, try and make the best choices (within your budget) for your health.

Explore new foods and drinks that decrease inflammation and increase your sparkle. Be comforted by the fact that every 7-10 years each cell in your body is replaced, so you're being given daily opportunities to replace old, damaged or diseased cells with new sparkle-filled ones. If this chapter has overwhelmed you, then just relax and take a deep breath. Try and reduce your stress a little, eat a few more veggies, make any other health-boosting changes* that feel easy and 'light' to do. Then, just enjoy your days and life because that's truly what'll get your sparkle back.

## 3 Small Sparkly Steps For Today…

1) Go and drink a large glass of water (with a small pinch of Celtic or Himalayan salt if you have some). If you don't have a water filter, go do some research on some of the best ones for your budget.

2) Try and work out what one of the biggest sources of dietary inflammation could be in your body – do you have dairy with every meal? Do you drink alcohol every night? Do you drink endless cups of coffee throughout the day? Now, either think how you could reduce just one of those things in a very small way today (to help reduce the inflammation in your body) OR add in something that you've learnt can help reduce inflammation.

3) Download the ThinkDirty App and look at some of the products that you use daily to see if once you've finished them there's a similar product with less chemicals you could swap to.

*Always consult your GP or holistic practitioner before you undertake any big changes to your diet – especially if you are currently receiving treatment or are on medication.*

# SPARKLE-FILLED
# ENERGY ACCOUNT

There's not one woman I know who doesn't want or need more energy. When you're low on energy, you're unable to live the way you want to and that affects your sparkle. Just as a car needs fuel to drive to all the places you want it to go, you need enough energy to fuel the life you want to live. I'm *not* talking about you having enough energy via 20 coffees to just scrape through your day wired or in a fog. I want you to have enough energy to do all the things you need *and* want to do in a day and feel good by the time you get into bed at night.

I want to show you that low energy and constant exhaustion isn't simply the natural result of being a woman, mum, or modern human. I want you to understand that if you have little to no energy every day then you should take that as a serious nod that your health and life isn't in the best sparkly shape. You've got to stop thinking that you must just "push through", "crack on" or see it as weakness or laziness if you're always exhausted because, this can set you up for a variety of mental and physical health problems long-term.

This chapter is to build upon what you've already learnt about how your energy levels predictably differ throughout your menstrual cycle and how if you start to adapt your life to the different rhythms (even just a little), you'll reap the benefits energy wise. You also now know about some of the foods and other things that can reduce your inflammation and therefore help increase your energy – because an inflamed body is usually an exhausted one too.

I want to help give you a deeper understanding of your energy, where it comes from, how you can protect it, and some of the other ways you can easily and cheaply boost it right away. I don't want you dragging yourself through your days when with a few changes you'll be able to skip or dance through them – if you so wish.

Don't get overwhelmed with all the tips and tricks in this section though. Just pick one or two things from this chapter that you can easily include in your life right away to help you feel a little better and sparklier. Then, over the next few weeks, look at another one or two things to work on and, before you know it, you'll have more energy than you've got right now, and therefore more sparkle.

## Your Energy Account

I'm sure you've heard the saying, "Time is money." Well, my saying is, "Energy is money." Just like your bank account, you have an 'energy account' that you make deposits into and withdrawals from every day. If not enough energy is being deposited into this account, and you constantly make withdrawals from it, you're going to be permanently 'overdrawn' and feel exhausted and crappy. Without fully understanding your energy account balance and transactions, you'll likely believe being totally knackered all the time is just how it is for you.

Now, think of a brand-new bank account and imagine that to live your happiest, sparkliest life, you'd need £100 deposited into it every day to spend. While you're sleeping, that £100 gets deposited into your bank account every night by your sparkly Fairy Godmother. At the start of each new day, you have all you need in your bank account to have a great day, with all your needs being met.

Every day you think you're only spending that £100. However, when you look at your bank account online before you go to bed each night, you see that you're always at least £400 overdrawn. That's a big difference in the amount of money you have and think you're spending compared to the amount you're actually spending.

So, what would you do in this situation? First, I'm guessing you'd check your account to make sure your £100 was being paid into your bank account every night. Next, you'd want to make sure you'd approved all of the payments going out of your account and also check nothing was being stolen. Then, you might look at your spending habits to see how many items you were spending money on that were unnecessary. Finally, you'd probably cut back on any needless spending so you could break even, stay in credit, and even start saving some money.

This process of investigation is *exactly* what's needed with your own 'energy account' if every day you never have enough energy and are always feeling totally 'spent'.

## Quick Energy Account Investigation

We're going to go through your energy account as if it's your bank account. Here's what our investigation, along with some credit-boosting strategies are going to cover:

1) How you can deposit more energy into your 'account' immediately so you can get back in 'energy credit' or at least break even.

2) See if you're aware of your spending habits and check if you've authorised all of the energy transactions you're making.

3) See if your energy is being stolen and how you can stop/ prevent that from happening.

4) Find out if your sparkly Fairy Godmother (i.e. your own body) is depositing energy overnight into your account.

## How To Deposit More Energy Into Your Account

Now, a good deal of your energy is either created or depleted by the things you eat – and we covered some of the biggies in the last chapter with regards to this. Remember, if you're energy is flagging, things like wonderful water, gorgeous greens and fabulous fats will all make some energy deposits into your energy account. Things like alcohol, sugar, processed foods, and stress will always steal from your energy account. However, there are numerous things that can boost or reduce your energy that have nothing to do with your diet but, are just as important and effective. Here's some of my faves…

## A Rest From Digesting

Okay, so this one is still on the subject of food but it's about you having a period of time where you rest from eating each day (don't panic, most of this will be when you're asleep!). Every time you eat (even one tiny morsel), your whole digestion system has to kick into action, which uses up a lot of energy. To eat one piece of food (sometimes when you're not even hungry) is like putting your whole washing machine on just for one pair of knickers. Ideally, you want to eat a 'full load' each time you ask your digestion to fire up.

In other words, try and eat enough during each meal to make yourself feel fully satisfied and truly nourished. Try not to be left hungry after a meal so that in an hour you're eating again and needing to get your digestive system working all over again. Adding in those fabulous fats and gorgeous greens to your meals should help you to feel fuller and satiated for longer. Also drinking enough wonderful water will help you to not confuse thirst for hunger, which is really easy to do when so many of us are dehydrated.

So, what I suggest to a lot of my clients to help keep their body in perfect sparkly balance (and not unnecessarily depleting their energy account) is to have at least 12 out of every 24 hours where they're *not* eating. This would naturally happen overnight if we lived more by our internal clocks and went to bed when it was dark. However, because we survive on less and less sleep these days by staying up late working, watching TV, or scrolling social media, we often also eat more in these nighttime hours when our body is meant to be resting. This increase of the hours we're eating in a day and decrease in the amount of sleep we get is a double blow to our energy account.

Since I've started not eating for 12 out of the 24 hours in a day I've realised, I do actually have more energy. I was someone who was always *hungry* – or so I thought. A lot of this was due to eating too much sugar, processed foods and not drinking enough water but, I'd also eat out of boredom – not knowing that my poor body was having to digest food that wasn't needed. However, since I've added more anti-inflammatory foods into my diet and am not constantly eating, my energy has significantly improved. Remember though, we're not men. Our appetites as women change over the month so don't ever rigidly stick to any eating method or plan (because these are normally done to suit the male cycle) and override what your body is asking from you. For instance, during my luteal or menstrual phase I may only fast for 10 hours or less, I just listen to my body and trust its cues.

Okay, so this is roughly what I do. If I have breakfast at 8am, I try to stop eating at the latest by 8pm each night – it's that simple. Whereas before food would be the "treat" I had each evening after a long day at work whilst I watched TV, now I make sure I eat enough throughout the day and enjoy other "treats" if I've got an evening on the sofa (more about this in the 'Sexy Sparkle' chapter).

Hear me when I say this is NOT a diet. This isn't about depriving myself or going to bed hungry. If my tummy rumbles because I'm working late and it wants peanut butter on toast then my god, I will have that peanut butter on toast. But, if I've eaten a big dinner, am bored, am delaying going to bed and want to eat just to fill some time, more often than not now, I'll let my digestive system (who has already worked a long day shift) rest. I'm just more intentional about eating more in the day and don't backload my eating to the evening.

Even if you try to do this 2 or 3 times a week, it'll likely help boost your energy and, more importantly, it'll let your body rest and gives it the chance to repair any damaged or diseased cells. 'Autophagy' is what this process is called and is your body's way of "cleaning" damaged cells to help prevent disease, regenerate cells, and prolong your life. Your body can't be digesting food and resting and repairing itself at the same time. It's why if an animal is sick or wounded, it'll naturally not eat and fast to help its body heal more quickly. This is what an overnight fast can help our body do too.

Some people do fast for longer than 12 hours. The one thing I'd say about that is even though lots of studies show how fasting can really benefit your health, most of the studies of its benefits are done on men (as most medical, sports and nutritional studies are). For women, you must understand that your body works differently than a man's and longer fasts (16 hours and over) have the potential to disrupt your hormones, fertility, and make your body store excess fat.

I believe for women nourishing our bodies lots in the day and then an overnight 12-hour fast is a great way to help increase energy, reduce inflammation, balance hormones, and reduce excess weight. This overnight fast is like that Sparkly

Fairy Godmother who helps put energy into your energy account whilst you sleep.

*Remember, make sure you consult with your doctor or holistic practitioner if making any big changes to your diet or lifestyle habits, especially if you're on medication or suffering from a severe illness. If you have suffered with or are suffering from an eating disorder, then please do not attempt to limit or restrict your food intake with any type of fast.*

## Rhythm Reset

Part of the reason for the onslaught of exhaustion in our present day is because we've gotten out of alignment with the natural rhythm of life. Women aren't widely taught about how their menstrual cycle affects their energy, appetite, and moods. We generally ignore the seasons of nature and the adjustments they call for in our lives and now, more than ever, the concept of night and day has been blurred. This disruption of our natural rhythm is severely messing with our health, happiness, and energy.

To feel your absolute best, you're meant to wake up with sunlight, be out in natural light throughout the day, and then rest and go to sleep when it gets dark. This natural rhythm was designed to help give you the energy you need for your daily tasks. However, it's been subverted with most people spending their days indoors with little to no natural light to signal to their body to feel awake. Then, at nighttime, you're likely bombarded with the bright lights from TVs, laptops, phones, artificial lighting in your home, and on your street – all of which signals to your body that it's daytime so you should stay awake. This reversal of your body's natural rhythm can leave you feeling more sluggish due to natural light (or the absence of it) being one of the main things that signals to your body to feel either awake or sleepy.

What you can do to try and bring your body back into balance is within 30 minutes of waking up (or it getting light outside), get out into natural daylight for at least 10 minutes and look at the sky (not directly at the sun though) – you can do this while you have your morning drink or if you're lucky, before the rest of your house wakes up. Even if it's not sunny, this hit of natural daylight will still boost your body. If you have a garden or some grass outside your house and want an extra energy-boosting, anti-inflammatory hack as you do your 10 minute sparkle-boosting sky stare, then try and do a little bit of 'grounding' (go look up it's health benefits). It's basically just having your feet on the natural ground (no shoes or socks allowed) so, if you've got a garden or some grass outside where you live then that's perfect. Sounds bonkers, yet this easy energy boost has been scientifically proven to reduce inflammation and increase your energy. There's a reason you feel so good when you paddle in the sea, have your feet on soft grass or walk across the sand, it's actually energising your cells.

Consider making a pledge to yourself that the natural light in the sky will hit your eyes before the artificial light of your phone does. Exposure to more natural daylight can help keep your mood, appetite, and hormones balanced. Waking up and feeling awake is due to cortisol being secreted. The more natural light you take in during the day (especially in the morning), the more cortisol and serotonin (the happy hormone) is produced – which means the more awake, alert, and even happy, you'll feel in the morning and during the day. Can you imagine feeling awake, alert, and happy in the mornings? It *is* possible.

Throughout the day try and get outside as much as you can – even just for 5 minutes here and there to walk a few steps, look at the sky, and take in some deep breaths of fresh air. This'll help boost your daytime energy and keep you feeling awake. It'll also help you sleep better at night too because serotonin is needed for your body to produce your sparkly sleep hormone – melatonin. In other words, you need the release of your 'daylight hormones' to release your 'sleepy hormone'.

I realised the power of natural light when I was in Las Vegas with my brother a few years ago. It was nighttime and we'd been out for dinner and I was super sleepy as we'd had a long day travelling. My brother asked if we could visit one of the casinos as it was on the way back to our hotel. So, we went to look around it and were probably there for about an hour looking at all the crazy things going on inside. Then, he asked, "Do you want to go back to the hotel now if you're tired?"

Now, I'm not someone who will ever pass up the opportunity to go to my bed, but I felt unusually energised considering an hour before I was dragging my feet like a grumpy toddler. We got chatting to someone inside the casino who was as equally bright-eyed as me considering the time, and she explained that casinos invest huge amounts of money on creating the right light needed to keep people feeling awake, alert, and not going to bed (so they keep gambling). The sneaky casino people had replicated morning daylight at night in the building, enabling cortisol and serotonin to be released. They'd also made sure there were no windows so people inside don't see when it's dark outside, which would signal the release of melatonin and make people start to feel sleepy – hence why I was no longer desperate for my bed.

Natural daylight is a powerful energy account booster so make sure you get it as early on in your day as possible and then as much as possible throughout your day. Don't let technology or modern living hi-jack the health and sparkle-boosting benefits that living by natural light and your natural rhythm can bring.

## Marvelous Movement

Sometimes our lives become sluggish and sedentary so gradually we don't even realise we're often sat down for most of the day, week, or month. I like to try and think of daily ways to move my body and movement to me isn't exercise. Exercise feels like something I've been told to do as a woman so I can look a certain way, lose weight, or "tone up". Whereas movement to me feels like something that can be fun, energising, and is what my body needs and was designed to do. Movement can be easily aligned with the things I enjoy most in life as opposed to forcing myself to do a form of exercise I don't enjoy.

There are obviously loads of reasons why you should move your body more if you're someone who's sat down for a lot of the day. One of the most important reasons is because a large percentage of your make up is water. Just like a still pool of water becomes stagnant, full of green sludge, and attracts nasty bugs if it doesn't ever move or flow – the same can happen to your body. It can also become "stagnant", which creates the right environment for fatigue, and disease.

If you're not used to moving your body regularly, you don't need to go crazy. Often we don't start any form of movement because we think, "I don't have time to go to the gym for an hour so, I just won't bother doing anything." Or, "I'm so unfit and I just don't have the energy to do what it'll take to improve my fitness." But, even just a little bit more movement than what you're currently doing will produce results. Just stand up right now, stretch your arms, twist your body from side to side, and sit back down again. You've already just boosted your body and energy and stopped it from feeling super stagnant and sluggish.

Various studies have shown that your risk of getting degenerative diseases can be dramatically reduced with regular movement – namely the sort that gets your skin sweating and heart pumping faster. Also, many people suffering from depression have testified to the fact that as little as 20 minutes of movement 3-4 times per week has boosted their energy and mood. So, think of types of movement that increase your excitement not exhaustion when you think about them. Something like going for a brisk walk with your favourite friend (even better if it's in an area with lots of nature) or dancing in your kitchen while you cook dinner all count.

I find with my clients that there seems to be two camps of women with regards to movement – those that overdo it and exercise daily regardless of where they are in their cycle or how they feel, and those that do very little if anything. The former women are often championed for ignoring their bodies and "cracking on" but, this ignoring the need for rest and how their cycle affects them can be as damaging, inflammatory and stressful as not doing any movement.

I had a friend of mine say to me once, "I could never get a dog. That means I'd have to walk it every day." I looked at her and said, "You know we're meant to walk everyday right? Not just dogs." We both laughed as we realised that people know dogs need daily or twice daily walks but somehow think humans don't – well we do!

So, follow where you are in your cycle to work out how much and what types of movement will boost your body. If you're currently doing very little movement, start small with 5 minutes a day, 3-4 times a week. Vary it so you don't get bored. And relish the extra glow, energy, and sparkle that more movement (at the right time of your menstrual cycle) can bring you.

## Your Sparkle Society

I often see the inspirational quote, "Stay close to people who feel like sunshine." My take on that is, "Hang around with people who make you feel super sparkly." If your energy and sparkle are struggling right now, then a quick way to boost them is to seek out people who you feel effortlessly energised after seeing. People who are grateful, encouraging, and those following their own passions and purpose are usually great energy-boosters. Likewise, limit your time with people who leave you feeling drained. Be especially selective when your energy is low, like when you're ill, your work is emotionally demanding or just before or on your period.

This week I was due on my period but had to travel for two hours to an appointment. My energy was really low and after my appointment I was even more tired. A friend who lived near to where my appointment was had asked that we go for lunch. Now, I'd seen that I would be in the low energy phase of my cycle, I knew that both the travel and the appointment would further deplete my energy account however, I knew that this friend always adds to my energy account so I agreed to lunch with her. When she saw me she did a little dance on the street (btw find friends who'll do a dance on the street when they see you), I just gave a lackluster wave and said, "Sorry I can't dance, I'm tired." We ate and chatted for two hours, and I felt as if I'd been given an energy transplant. As we waved goodbye, I did a little dance because my energy and sparkle had been boosted by being around this friend.

Make a list of the people that you feel energised just thinking about spending time with, and those who make you feel tired at the thought of being with them for an hour. Try and see the energy-boosting peeps far more than those that constantly drain you. I'm not saying only have positive people around you and get rid of the rest, but instead be acutely aware of your energy account and understand who affects your credit in a positive or negative way. Create your own 'sparkle society' of people who you know consistently boost your mood, energy, and sparkle whenever you spend time with them.

## Sparkle-Up Your Surroundings

It's not only the people you surround yourself with on a daily basis that'll affect how much energy you have and how brightly your sparkle can shine. It's the other physical things around you, too. Have you thought about how your home, the place where you spend so much of your time, looks, and feels? Is it overrun with clutter and things for your business, kids, or partner? Do you have a purely functional home, or have you included items and areas that inspire, uplift, and boost you? If you don't like your home and instead spend time just dreaming of your perfect house, then it's time to spruce up and add some sparkle to where you live right now. This will give you an immediate lift and boost your energy.

I always make sure that if a client is really struggling with tiredness or apathy for their life that they create at least one room or area in their home that reflects their true self and the things they love in life. Look around your living space – is there a room, area, or even a shelf that lights you up? No? Well, it's time to do a little re-arranging so that any time you feel uninspired, overwhelmed or sparkle-less, you can go to this energy-boosting area and remember who you are and what makes you happy.

For years, I didn't buy or display anything glittery or chintzy because I thought my husband had better taste than I did when it came to interiors. I was hiding an important part of me for fear of people thinking it was tacky or childish. However, one day I looked around our house and couldn't see any of my personality in our home – sure, it looked stylish but to me it was a little sparkle-less and that was affecting my energy. I realised that by not having any fun, sparkly, or quirky things to look at and uplift me every day that I felt a little suppressed and sad about my surroundings.

So, now I've dotted some my favourite things around the house especially in rooms I spend a lot of time in (hello pineapple lamp in the kitchen, fluffy throw in the bedroom, and roller-skating rabbit picture in the lounge). I've also decorated my office and spare room in the house so it totally reflects me – I have a picture covered in fake, brightly-coloured flowers. I have two pairs of my sparkliest heels on display. A trophy I won in a roller-skating competition decades ago takes pride of place, and there's a bookcase full of books that I adore and inspire me. I look at this room and it makes me smile and gives me a little boost when I'm busy. It reminds me of some of the things that I love the most, and just thinking about those things energises me.

You don't have to spend a lot of energy and money having a sort out and sparkling up your surroundings. You may already have all the items you love and need to create an energising space just for you. Why not start with just a 'sparkle shelf' or corner of one room and make it 100% yours. Don't hide your love of colour just because you've been told it's not chic. Don't hide a picture that you adore because everyone else makes fun of it. Don't think because you live in a city you can't have your love of the sea all around you now. Don't hide your records even if you haven't made time to play them in years. Make an area that you're reminded of your most joyous, sparkly self in, where all the other labels you might carry like "mum", "wife", "business owner", "cleaner", and "stress-head" are not welcome or reflected. Create a space that fills you with happiness and get rid of any items or clutter that drag you down and dull your sparkle by looking at them (yes, time to get rid of those grey knickers with a hole in!).

The final thing you can do to boost your energy in your surroundings is to play music you love. Whenever you have low energy and are feeling a bit 'blah', think of three of your most favourite songs and play them back to back. In fact, do that now (or if you're reading this before bed, do it first thing tomorrow morning). I'm telling you, your whole body will feel better (especially if you move it as well) once it hears your magic sparkle-boosting music. This tip is actually part of my '7-day Sparkle Boosting Strategy' that you'll get for free if you sign up to my newsletter at www.womenwithsparkle.com/ subscribe.

Your home is meant to be (or at least have areas that can be) your 'sparkle sanctuary'. If it doesn't feel like that, take the smallest action to change it – de-clutter one drawer, fill one shelf with items you love, chuck out the mug with a chip or the jeans that don't fit, and make playing uplifting music a regular occurrence in your home. Just wait and see how much your mental and physical energy improves by your sparkled-up surroundings.

## Happy Habits

One of my all-time favourite tips to help you boost your energy account and sparkle is… you have to go roller-skating! I use roller-skating as an example, of course, but I want you to think of the things that you did when you were at your happiest, free-est and sparkliest – even if this was decades ago. And for me, the way I tap into that happy, sparkly, 7 year old girl who thought she could achieve anything, be anything and just loved life, is to do some of her favourite things without worrying that at 41, I shouldn't be. Things like roller-skating.

We lose our sparkle as women when we do less and less of the things our soul truly loves and more of the things that we feel we should. These "shoulds" often make us feel put upon, sad, bored, and subdued. If your day involves doing the dishes and ignoring the fact that dancing energises you, then make a change asap. If that means putting your favourite music on and dancing *while* doing the dishes, then so be it.

If you run around after others all day but truly love the feeling you get from going for an actual run, then get serious about your sparkle, go in your lunch break or get someone else to hold the fort for 30 minutes and head outside for that run. Even knowing you can do this once a week will boost your sparkle. If you love to cook but your work leaves you so busy and tired that you end up eating something processed and quick each night, plan ahead and make sure at least once or twice a week you have the ingredients to cook a sparkly (and speedy if necessary) supper for yourself to enjoy. Your energy and sparkle depend on you doing at least one thing that lights you up every day. Here's a simple equation to boost your energy and sparkle:

ADD one thing to your day that lights you up
SUBTRACT one or more unhappy habits from your day
this EQUALS a more energised and sparkle-filled you.

Some of the things that I try and do daily, weekly, or monthly because they energise me and make my soul sparkle are:

- sipping my cup of tea slowly
- being around dogs
- getting a hug from a loved one
- going to a dance class
- having a lie-in
- being in nature
- having a bath
- and roller-skating!

For a long time, I'd replaced a lot of those happy habits with unhappy ones. I was working in a dreary office, forcing myself to work out in a gym with no windows, never being in nature or around animals, having showers instead of baths, and thinking I was too old or it was too embarrassing for me to roller-skate. It's no wonder my sparkle was a mere flicker instead of a burning flame and my energy account was so depleted (and thoroughly overdrawn) that I was dragging myself through most of my days.

So, what are the things you used to do at your happiest and you don't do anymore? Singing? Going out with your friends? Being silly? Being arty? Knitting? Kickboxing? Roller-skating? Painting? Cooking? Walking? Tap dancing?

Ignore the insecurities or the voice (or other people) that might say you're "too old to do that", to pursue your favourite hobbies, past-times, or passions – you're not! Those things are a big deal when it comes to you feeling youthful, happy, healthy, and having more energy. Follow the path of the things that truly light you up when you think about them because they'll lead you straight back to your vibrancy, energy, and sparkle.

Now we've hopefully found a few ways that you can boost your energy account. Let's see what else we need to look at...

**Energy Transactions – Have You Approved Them All?**

You may not realise this but EVERYTHING you do spends your energy – from worrying about something, digesting your food, scrolling social media, to cooking dinner. Using the same idea of you having £100 to spend from your energy account every day, let's look at some of the daily transactions you might be making, many of which you might not be aware of:

• Wake up to an alarm clock that puts your body in an immediate state of shock – £2 of energy
• Get your kids up and get them ready – £3 of energy

• Make a cup of coffee and look at the chipped mug that you hate – £1 of energy

• Worry about a work problem – £4 of energy

• Unload the dishwasher – £2 of energy

• Put washing on and hang out previous load – £4 of energy

• Get yourself showered – £2 of energy

• Think about what to wear – £2 of energy

• Get dressed – £1 of energy

• Make breakfast and eat it – £5 of energy (remember, digesting food uses up a good amount of energy, which is why you can feel sleepy after a big meal)

• Walk and feed the dog – £6 of energy

• Argue with your partner and keep thinking about the argument – £9 of energy

• Sort out a work problem – £6 of energy

• Make some work calls – £5 of energy

• Reply to personal text messages and emails – £2 of energy

• Think about replying to all the other personal texts and emails from the past days – £2 of energy

• Pay a credit card bill and get stressed about the outstanding amount – £2 of energy

• Think about what to cook for dinner and what you need to buy – £4 of energy

- Scroll through Instagram and feel rubbish in comparison to others – £3 of energy
  - Buy lunch – £4 of energy
  - Eat lunch – £5 of energy
  - Think about all the housework that needs doing – £2 of energy
  - Order a birthday present for your friend – £3 of energy
  - Call your sick parent – £4 of energy
  - Worry about your sick parent – £10 of energy
  - Watch the news and be overwhelmed by it – £4 of energy
  - Look in the mirror and worry about your weight – £3 of energy

Before you've even reached the afternoon, you've already spent your daily 'energy budget' of £100. Add into the mix you probably haven't had enough sleep or nutritious food (which is like starting your day with an energy deficit of £50), or maybe you're on or due on your period (again, this'll mean your energy budget is starting at a much lower level), not forgetting, there's the mental exhaustion of being a woman which means you're constantly bombarded with the idea that on top of all the things you need to do day to day you're also meant to be perfect/happy/slim/sexy/successful/thoughtful/positive/ look after everyone around you. It's too much!

Do you now start to see why you're feeling pretty exhausted most days? Your 'energy account', like your bank account, has a daily limit and you've been spending it like it's unlimited.

## Emergency Energy Account Overdraft

Of course, an 'emergency energy account overdraft' does exist. So, for the times when you've spent all your energy but it's vital you keep going, you can. However, like a normal overdraft, this is meant to be a back-up for emergencies like moments of extreme stress, grief, or hard times. You're not meant to live off of your emergency energy account overdraft. This is because the interest rates of most overdrafts are usually pretty high and if this is how you live, you may need help managing your money more efficiently. It's the same with your energy account overdraft – you're not meant to live out of it the whole time as the high interest rates of stress cause inflammation which'll damage your body and mind.

Your emergency energy account overdraft is what's known as your body's 'fight or flight' system that kicks in to help you in stressful situations. It's meant to be there as a back-up to help you run from an attack or help someone urgently in need. Stress hormones, which are like your body being given an emergency cash injection of £500 to spend immediately, are pumped into your body to momentarily energise you. However, once the emergency is over, your body is meant to be able to move out of this high stress state, live from its normal 'energy account', and pay back the overdraft.

Too many women live from their energy overdraft all day, every day, consistently pumping stress hormones into their body and ignoring their body's desperate cries to be brought back into balance. Too often women ignore the 'no funds left in your energy account' message their body gives them and simply have another coffee, something with lots of sugar in and "crack on".

But, if your bank sent you a message to say you have no money left in your bank account and even your overdraft limit was nearing its limit, would you ignore it and keep spending money regardless? Most probably not. But, when it comes to your energy account and the messages your body gives you (thirst, hunger, tiredness etc), you'll often just keep on spending.

I know you think it doesn't matter if you're tired because you're spending your energy on others who need you – your work, partner, kids, family, friends, pets. But, would it matter if you told the bank that they didn't need to worry about you overspending as you weren't buying things for yourself, you were buying things for other people? No, it wouldn't matter. Spending beyond your limits is spending beyond your limits regardless of the well-meaning intentions behind it.

This constant over-spending when you have low or no energy is super harmful to your health and sparkle because it increases inflammation, imbalances your hormones and suppresses your immune system. You're not meant to just keep hammering your energy overdraft with another coffee or processed snack because if you don't take time to pay back your 'energy overdraft' with extra rest, calm thoughts, and good food, your body will become chronically inflamed.

Constant inflammation in your body (which may show up as acne, eczema, painful periods, joint pain or another persistent symptom) is like a warning from the bank that you're in serious debt. A constantly stressed out and inflamed body ends up spending even *more* of your precious energy trying to reduce that inflammation (with the hope of preventing serious diseases in your body). This means there's little or no energy left to feel good or do all the things you'd love to have energy for. Your body should be able to produce all the natural energy you need, but if you keep pushing it into its overdraft with things like constant stress, caffeine and sugar and not resting enough, your body will get the message that it doesn't need to produce this amount of energy for you anymore.

Women can be so unkind to themselves. They can be exhausted, suffering from a range of physical and emotional problems, and yet still they push themselves to keep going. If you saw a horse that had just run a race, has shaky legs and was near collapsing – would you just want someone to give it a strong coffee, whip it, and tell it to "crack on"? If a child was teary and tired and all they wanted to do was take a short nap – would you give them a packet of biscuits and tell them, "You can't rest, there's work to get done today"? No, you wouldn't because treating an animal or a child like that would be beyond cruel and abusive.

So, please stop being cruel and abusive to yourself when you're exhausted and needing to rest. Use that energy overdraft for emergencies and life's unexpected happenings. Don't compensate for the fact you have nothing left in your energy account because you've not deposited any extra good credit in your account (good food, water, rest etc) and stop overspending what you don't have.

## Energy Account Stealers

Let's take a little look at some of the most common things that may be stealing from your 'energy account' and could be keeping you in your 'energy overdraft'. Think of these things like unauthorised direct debits. Even getting rid of one or two of them will help boost your 'energy account' and bring you a feeling of increased health and sparkle.

## Beware Of Scammers

In the last chapters we've talked lots about how your daily choice of food and drink is one of the easiest ways you can increase or decrease your energy account. However, I want you to know that if you don't find the idea of more water, fabulous fats, and gorgeous greens as mouth-watering as me asking you to increase your intake of doughnuts, crisps and pizza, then there's a really valid reason for that. And it's not that you're naturally a lazy, greedy, unhealthy overeater who has no willpower to stick to a diet (which is the message too many women have been getting for years from the weight loss and fitness industries).

It isn't that you need to "try harder" to enjoy the "right" foods and ignore the "wrong" foods. Just trying harder to want chicory instead of chips, or chard instead of chocolate, isn't going to cut it. The game has been rigged against you. You're being scammed (with food science) out of your energy.

Believe it or not, your body knows when you've had enough to eat and when to stop eating. It also knows which foods will give it energy and which are not so great. It has systems that stop you wanting to overeat overly salty or sweet foods because your body knows you only need a small amount of those things.

Have you even thought about why if you're craving something fatty, sweet, or salty that you don't reach for butter, raw sugar, or salt? Because if you did, you'd only have a small amount of those foods and then your body would make you not want any more. However, these natural systems in your body have been hi-jacked.

Firstly, foods and emotions from your upbringing play a part in how your body craves certain types of foods. Since you were a child, you were most likely given certain foods as a treat or a reward. This results in your taste buds and brain chemistry being trained to favour these foods. You'll have watched adverts and programs where fizzy drinks, sweets, and sugary cereals were all there when fun was being had. You would've experienced some of your most sparkly times as a kid likely surrounded by cakes and crisps, not kale and carrots.

So, growing up you were constantly associating some foods with pleasure and others with pain (anyone else forced to stay at the table and finish their vegetables when all you wanted to do was be playing outside or watching TV?). Some foods you'll still associate with comfort and happiness, and others with being "forced" to be "good" or include them in your diet. Just be aware of the emotions you have around certain foods.

A more sinister reason for your wanting to select French fries instead of French beans to accompany your meals are that food companies know how your body and brain work better than you do. These companies use that to their advantage to keep you buying and craving their products. Some food companies use scientific information about how your brain lights up when eating certain food combinations and have deliberately made their foods "hyper-palatable". This means you'll always feel a great amount of pleasure when eating them and want more.

You have a reward pathway in your brain that releases dopamine – a super-duper, feel good neurotransmitter linked with feelings of pleasure. Certain foods and food combinations stimulate this reward pathway, which is also stimulated and "rewarded" by addictive drugs like cocaine. The trouble is that no natural foods release the high levels of dopamine and 'highs' that cleverly created processed foods do. And processed foods steal from your energy account (due to them often containing things that cause inflammation).

Food companies often work with specialist consultants and food chemists to combine magical combinations of sugar, salt, and fat (usually with starch) because they know this is a combination that can "light up" the pleasure, reward, and addictive pathways of your brain.

If you find yourself excessively eating or thinking about certain food items, don't just blame yourself. Look at the ingredients! They've probably been engineered to contain the combination of sugar, salt, and fat to give you a dopamine hit. Know that these ingredients won't always be labelled clearly with those names and will often be hidden by other words/ terms. There are also certain food additives (like MSG) that give you the feeling that you *need* these foods and you're often unable to stop wanting, thinking about, or eating them.

Lots of research is done when creating new foods or drinks to establish the "bliss point" for them. The bliss point is when a substance has the right amount of sugar, salt, fat, or combination of all three to make you keep coming back for more. The people creating these foods know that a too sweet, salty, or fatty taste will be a turn off (hence why our body doesn't crave the spoonfuls of sugar, salt, or fat). The highest amount of this combination before it tastes too sweet, salty, or fatty is the "bliss point" and it's always rigorously pursued, tested, and researched on people before a product is launched. For more information on this, read the fascinating book *The End of Overeating* by Dr David A. Kessler.

So, if this clever chemistry has left you feeling exhausted by your diet and powerless around food, don't worry. You now have the insider knowledge you need. I like to think of these foods like a drop-dead gorgeous guy at a friend's party who's flirting with you, flattering you, and making you feel pretty excited about his attention. You're just about to fall for his charms and spend the night with him when you remember that before the party your best friend warned you about him. She told you that this guy has studied how to charm women and says the same things to all women to titillate and flatter them (only to give the ones who do go home with him a variety of not so lovely diseases). Armed with that knowledge, you'd likely end your flirtation with him and move away to chat to someone else who wasn't artificially creating a connection between you.

The good news is you can retrain your taste buds and brain to help take back control of your food choices, energy, and super-boost your sparkle. Instead of letting the sneaky tricks of food scientists dictate your day with always needing certain snacks or fast food, know that there are choices you can make to rewire your brain and break food addictions. The more you focus on adding in more water, fabulous fats, and gorgeous greens as well as lots of other colourful fruits and veggies, the less you'll consistently fall for and crave the inflammatory charms of the processed sugar, salt, and fat products that are scamming you and stealing from your energy account.

## Are People Stealing From You?

I know we've talked about your 'sparkle society' of people to help boost your energy account. I want to stress the importance of the people in your life because they also have a big influence on how much energy gets taken needlessly from you every day. It might be a family member that calls you multiple times a day and you think you "have" to pick the phone up. Or maybe the friend who always wants a text back asap so you can help her with something. Or it's the client who thinks you should be on call 24/7. Or the colleague who's so negative that after a five-minute conversation with them you feel utterly drained.

If you don't fully authorise these energy transactions, then you're letting people steal from your energy account. Now, if you have lots of energy to spare, then this is fine. However, I'm guessing, like me, you don't. You just perhaps feel too bad to say no to them. Or perhaps you think this is just the way things have to be for you to be a good daughter, friend, nice colleague, or person. These transactions have to stop!

If you have little to no energy most days, then you don't have any spare to keep giving away. Your energy is precious, so start making a note of where or with whom too many of these transactions are occurring and think of ways to put some boundaries in so that it's not always you taking the hit from your energy account. If you'd not let the people around you dip into your bank account whenever they needed some money, don't let them do the same with your energy account.

## Your energy drains quicker than your phone's battery…

… and yet you probably charge your phone more often. Plus, your phone could be part of the problem.

Did you know that you were meant to be in control of your phone? Have you realised that your phone is now actually in control of you? Do you use its alarm to wake you up? Do you jump up and read a text straight away if you hear it beep? Is it the last thing you look at night before you go to bed and first thing when you wake up? Do you often ignore loved ones and things around you because your focus is on the lights on that screen?

There's no shame here – this was me! But, after looking at the things stealing from my energy account, I realised that my phone was one of those things.

I'd thought that being on my phone was relaxing and helped me wind down after a busy day. The reality of the fact was that it was keeping me busy. It was over-stimulating my mind which signaled to my body that I wasn't relaxed – everything from looking at 1000 different people's lives on

Instagram, to being tempted to online shop just because the app is there and adverts pop up. I also wasn't able to watch a film with my husband without feeling the need for a sneaky scroll. I realised I was addicted! And addictions drain your energy because you're always thinking about what you're addicted to. I realised my phone had started to own me and be in charge of my time and waste my energy. Time I could be using to improve my health, write this book or truly rest.

Let's be real for a moment. Phones and social media can be a fantastic tool in life BUT you have to realise that anything free usually has a purpose to make money. Instagram (which is my social media app of choice) makes money by "watching" your habits and "gently" placing ads right in front of you based on the things it knows you like. It's actually super creepy when you think about it (especially because someone who works in the industry told me they can use your phone microphone to listen to your conversations, pick out words and again place ads you'll be interested in. This would make sense as to why the other day I was talking about an electric toothbrush and then 'hey presto' electric toothbrush ads were appearing on my social media feed!)

I also found out the other day – which I shouldn't be surprised by, but lots of these platforms employ huge teams of people whose sole job it is to find ways to make you spend more time on these apps. They're getting paid big bucks to understand your brain to make you spend your time, energy, and money on something that seems fun without realising how much of your time and energy are actually being wasted and stolen in front of your eyes.

Many of the apps that we use every day use the same psychology and technology combinations that are used on gambling apps – with the aim being to keep you on there as long as possible so you spend your time, energy and eventually money. I've heard that many of the people who create or own some of the biggest social media platforms wouldn't want their own kids to use them because they know the effect they have on your mind.

There's no denying phones are a useful tool. However, the 24/7 access to information can be quite stressful. It's like phones have become part of our bodies. Phones are always in our hands or are always in our pockets or resting on our laps. We weren't born with a phone attached to our hand, therefore I'm guessing that's because we don't need it attached to our hand for our best health and life. We need to try and get a little distance and freedom from our phones so their constant ringing and pinging (which all create an energy account depleting stress response) or lure to scroll news or social media doesn't waste energy we don't have to spare.

I've started having some days where I decide to not always have my phone on or near me so I can take ownership back of my body, mind, time, and energy. I want my phone as a tool I use, not a compulsion that I can't be without. Just try to create a little distance between yourself and your phone and see if you find some hours and energy you didn't realise you had. Also, see being on your phone as 'energy phone banking' where you're either letting your energy drain away with the things you look at and do whilst you're on it. Or you can use it to learn and truly connect with people who inspire, uplift, and teach you.

This has been a real journey of learning for me with my phone. I came off Instagram for a month to prove to myself that my business and world wouldn't fall apart if I did and BOOM! I had more energy! My business didn't suffer. I truly engaged with my husband, I read the books I'd had in a pile by my bed, I went to bed earlier – all the things I thought I was too busy to do before when actually, I was just too distracted. I've started to put myself – not app developers or my phone – back in control of my time and energy. What's one way you could start to do this too?

## Your Passion And Purpose

Believe it or not, you were created with a purpose – one which energises you (even if it scares you or you don't believe it's possible) when you think about it. You have certain passions that fill you with energy and excitement, and are there as guideposts to your purpose. If you're in a job you hate or work you don't care about, then you'll probably find this drains your 'energy account'. Don't get overwhelmed at the thought of trying to find a new job or following your passions and purpose just yet if this feels too huge.

Just concentrate on finishing this book and getting your sparkle back. Then it'll feel like a much easier, more natural thing for you to do and think about. But know this! There's work you could be doing (even if it's not your main job right now) that you'd feel delighted, not depleted by. Work that'd make you feel sparkly, not sad. Work that you were born to do and are not bribed to do by a wage.

I trust that by the time you've finished this book you'll have more confidence, energy, and belief in yourself than you had at the start. This will help you remember that your passions are linked with your purpose and you're being reminded to pursue them. The added bonus is, there'll be more energy waiting for you, when you start working on the things you truly love in life.

## Is Your Energy Being Paid Into Your Account Overnight?

Getting a good night's sleep is (along with drinking enough wonderful water) *the* most basic foundation needed for your health and sparkle. Every night, if you're getting a decent enough sleep, your body (your very own Sparkly Fairy Godmother) repairs and restores many things in your body that play a role in how much energy you have.

At different times of life, your sleep may be unavoidably disrupted (work, kids, illness, hormonal changes etc). I'm not dismissing how difficult your circumstances might be or how a certain condition may be affecting your sleep, but you *have* to get creative and fight for the vital deposits into your energy account from sleep that you need. Your mental and physical health relies on it. Even the smallest amount of extra sleep will make a big difference to your energy levels, and therefore sparkle.

Get help to get to the root cause of your sleep disruption and don't give up until someone or something helps improve it. Don't just think that terrible sleep is the price you pay for being a mum, having a successful job, or being a woman. Here's my tips to help you get some more sleep if you're currently starved of it. I'm giving you this advice as someone who's sleep is currently being disturbed nightly. But no matter how long it takes, I'm determined to find the sleep and rest my body needs from somewhere and not just "put up" with it (which is the message lots of women get).

- **Ask for help.** This is a biggie that too many women forget to do! Whether it's your kids, pets, or a worried mind that's robbing you of important sleep, ask friends, family, an expert, read books, and get whatever support you need to get more sleep. Don't just joke that you're always tired. Don't think that just because other women are exhausted you should be. Don't just run your body on caffeine and sugar to make up for the exhaustion and damage your health in the process. Fight for yourself in the same way you would a loved one who you saw was in desperate need of more sleep.

- **Change your curtains** to black out ones if outside lights are disturbing your sleep. Similarly, because light can affect your sleep quality, don't have lights from phones or other technology in your bedroom.

- **Have a warm bath** before bed. Add in some Epsom salts, lavender, or frankincense essential oil to your bath to help your mind and body relax.

- **Turn the temperature down** in your house in the evening so it's cooler than normal to help you sleep more deeply.

- **Don't be on your phone or laptop 60 minutes before bed.** If you have to be, invest in some blue/green light blocking glasses (like the ones in the 'Sparkly Recommendations' section).

- **Visit a holistic practitioner** who can talk you through any sleep problems and help suggest some supplements that could help you sleep if you're struggling with an illness, hormonal shifts, have a busy mind or anxious thoughts that make it difficult for you to sleep well.

- **Consider relocating/seek other advice** if where you're living means that your sleep is constantly disturbed in some way. I know this sounds drastic, but poor sleep directly affects your health by limiting your body's ability to repair itself. If you're always being disturbed by your neighbours and surroundings and you've exhausted (excuse the pun) all other avenues, then moving or trying to get professional help to solve the problem is preferable to damaging your precious health.

And if you *really* can't get a good night's sleep, then let me introduce you to sleep's wonderful relation called 'rest'. If you're not able to sleep well, then rest is essential to keep you in health and able to produce some form of natural energy and sparkle. The trouble is getting adequate rest gets a bad rap.

It goes against the 'badge of honour' of being busy. Showing that you're being busy has always been linked with being successful, important, or at least valuable as a woman. Rest on the other hand is thought to be a luxury or what ill, old, or lazy people do. I know you think being knackered is part and parcel of being a woman or getting older – many of us had this modelled to us by our parents or other women around us – but, it's not meant to be that way. Rest isn't meant to feel like a distant dream that's laden with guilt.

Since I got ill and now understand the need for your body to experience rest, I take resting very seriously. I do all I can to increase my times of 'rejuvenating rest' so that my energy account gets enough income to get me through my days and I ignore the "it's alright for you" crew who like to comment when I proudly say that I've been resting or napping. I want to start rebranding napping as something that ninjas, not nanas, do. It shouldn't be something that's just reserved for holidays or when you're ill.

I'm a huge fan of *The Nap Ministry* by Trisha Hersey who has created an, "organisation that examines the liberating power of naps..." She believes that, "Rest is form of resistance and reparations" and I'm here for it! (Go follow @thenapministry on Instagram).

Arianna Huffington has done great research into sleep and why it's so needed – she even installed nap rooms in her fast-paced news offices as the scientific research showed naps created incredible results like lowering people's blood pressure, boosting their immune system, memory, learning abilities, as well as reversing the performance deteriorating effects of sensory overload. I highly recommend her book *The Sleep*

*Revolution* as she shows in detail the power, not pointlessness, of naps.

Proudly be a woman who takes mini naps and don't shame other women if you don't. The whole idea that you're meant to be awake/alert from the moment you wake up just isn't how the human body functions best. It's been said that the "pulse and pause" way of working where we do some work/activity (pulse) and then rest (pause) is much more suited to the human body and mind (and keeping them healthy) than the factory-workers mentality, where you wake up and work till your working hours are over.

Did you know that even a short 6-12-minute rest, whenever you can get one, will boost your energy levels? Just this brief moment to lie down, close your eyes, relax your body, and breathe deeply (with no phone, TV, or distractions around) can actually help reset your brain, body, and boost your energy. So, if a full night's sleep constantly eludes you, you refuse like an overtired toddler to nap, or you're thinking you'll only be able to recharge if you get a 2-week holiday, look to take 6-12 minutes of rest today. And keep repeating this – especially on your busiest days. You'll start to feel your body repay you with deposits of energy that you didn't have before and thought you needed a lot longer to get. Sleep and rest are such a key component of your health and happiness that it has to no longer be ignored or fantasised about. Your sleep and rest must now be prioritised on your journey to getting your sparkle back.

**Password Protected**

Your energy is one of the most precious resources that you have. Stop giving it away like it has no value and wondering why there's none left for you. Your online bank account has a password to protect it. Make sure you start protecting your 'energy account' in the same way and not giving everyone access to it. Stop doing more and more in your days. Stop saying "yes" to every request that comes your way. Protect empty days, hours, or minutes fiercely and don't just fill them because you think recharging is lazy and someone needs something from you. Stop thinking that it's always *your* energy that has to be spent when things need doing. If warning lights in your body are flashing with exhaustion, painful periods, weariness, teariness, anger, anxiety, a lack of sex drive etc, do an 'energy account' audit and start making some changes.

Spend time doing things that aren't always about others. Add in food and drinks that boost, not reduce, your energy. Do some things that make you feel like the best version of yourself and, for goodness sake, just rest! Once you understand your 'energy account', teach the people in your life about it so you can easily say, "I don't have the energy for that today because I've spent all that was in my account."

Decide you're not going to spend tomorrow's energy, health, and sparkle by overspending or overstretching yourself today. Let, "I'm not able to do that" be your updated password where before it was, "Yes, no problem". Do this and you'll soon start to feel your energy account break even and get some sparkly savings reserved just for you and the things you love (which btw will in turn give you more energy). Ignore the myth that being tired is just the way it is, there's so much more for you in this life my darling, but you'll need some more energy to be able to do it and get your sparkle back.

### 3 Small Sparkly Steps For Today…

1) Think about one thing you're going to try and add into your day to boost your energy account.
2) Think about one thing that steals your energy that you can remove today.
3) Go lie down, shut your eyes, take ten deep breaths, and rest for between 6-12 minutes and feel the huge benefits that such a short moment of rest can bring.

# SEXY SPARKLE

A big part of getting your sparkle back is getting back a feeling of sexiness. However, being or feeling sexy isn't the narrow idea we've been sold as women – it's not all high heels, lingerie, and actual sex. No, your 'Sexy Sparkle' isn't reliant on the ideas promoted by masculine ideals whereby a certain body type, clothes, or sexual activity is involved. We're talking about a type of feminine inner sexiness that can be seen or felt by the glint in your eyes, spring in your step, and aura that says, "I'm really turned on, and tuned in to myself and life right now." *That's* what your 'sexy sparkle' is, and I'm going to show you how to get it back.

## The Silent Health Crisis For Women That No One's Talking About

Let's start with a simple analogy. If you'd been held underwater for a long time and then came up to the surface – how would you breathe? You'd be gasping for air, wouldn't you? That's because your body knows how vital oxygen is for keeping you alive. Keep this image in your head because most women are starved of (and therefore 'gasping' for) a crucial supplement in their life that helps optimise their energy, joy, vitality, confidence, and sexy sparkle. So, what is it?

Well, it's Vitamin OYP. Its full name is Vitamin 'Oh Yes Plllease'. Okay, it's not actually a vitamin and I made that name up, but I love it being described as this because I often prescribe certain vitamins to my clients because they or their diets are deficient in them and its affecting their health, vitality and sparkle. However, as well as some of the most common vitamins many women are deficient in (like Vitamin B, C, D etc), most of my clients (because they're women) are severely deficient in Vitamin 'Oh Yes Plllease'. This deficiency is serious because it too reduces their health, vitality, and sparkle. I believe this 'supplement' is as needed and nutritious to your female body as any green smoothie or high-quality food supplement I recommend to my clients. You'll likely know this little health and sparkle booster by its street name which isn't Vitamin OYP, it's called *pleasure*.

This may sound crazy to you, but I believe and have seen in countless women's lives that pleasure is a necessary and a vital 'nutrient' for women's full health and sparkle. If you're not experiencing any form of genuine pleasure during your day, it means you'll be deficient and depleted in it. The side effects you might experience will leave you 'gasping' for it. This 'gasping' for pleasure can present itself as binge eating, binge online shopping, binging on social media, or anything else that might help satisfy the very natural and needed (not naughty) pleasure cravings of your female body. I know you think these behaviours are because you have no willpower or are just too lazy to make any changes to your life or habits but, the truth is, many of these sparkle-stealing behaviours can be the result of not understanding the cries of your body for pleasure that come from an important organ in your female body.

It's worth noting that pleasure isn't something luxurious reserved for the privileged or rich, and it's most certainly not just about sex (which the word is often associated with). Pleasure, and what the feeling of it does to your body and mind, is something that you need to help *protect* your mental and physical health. It actually helps reduce inflammation in your cells and therefore your body meaning your hormones are more balanced and your health is boosted. The reason this is such important news is because as we've learnt from the other sparkly chapters so far – if we're wanting to have better periods, moods, more energy, balance our hormones, and help prevent serious diseases like cancer and heart disease – then we must do all we can to reduce chronic inflammation in our bodies. Pleasure can help you do this!

## Pleasure Propaganda

As a woman, you'll have likely been taught from a young age that pleasure isn't a necessity in your daily life and is something that has to be earned. Whether it's a nap, a night away, a cup of tea in peace or a slice of chocolate cake – none of these things usually come without you having to barter, trade, beg or believe it's not okay for you to want or have them. If you experience any form of pleasure, you'll likely feel selfish and obliged to make up for it through guilt. Many of us will have voices in our head saying things like, "Eaten a slice of cake? I hope you're going for a run now to burn it off!" Or you try over-compensating in other situations with, "You let me take a 10-minute nap? I'm so grateful. I didn't deserve it when there were other things to be done. I'll now make up for it by doing everything around the house."

Pleasure (just like breathing air or drinking water) isn't something for women to earn, justify, hide, deny, feel guilty about, or only experience on special occasions. There's been some consistent pleasure propaganda for hundreds of years that's dished out through schools, the media, families, corporations, and religious institutions that overtly or covertly have taught the idea that "good", virtuous women should endlessly care for and serve others, not themselves. "Good", "virtuous", and "pleasing" women (I feel nauseous just writing those descriptions) shouldn't 'indulge' in their own pleasure because it's seen as selfish, gluttonous, excessive, promiscuous, and unspiritual.

Women who like their bodies and allow themselves to experience any form of pleasure have usually been shamed and portrayed by negative stereotypes – slutty, selfish, heartless, greedy etc – because a woman who believes she deserves and takes control of her own pleasure cannot be easily controlled by others. This notion of a woman who values and seeks her own pleasure is frightening to institutions or families (ok let's face it, most of the world) that've long survived on the control or suppression of women. Many of these structures are based on women denying their own needs and always addressing the needs of others – and more often than not, never asking or getting paid for this service.

So, shall we have a little fun and start undoing the cultural programming that labels any woman who takes care of herself and seeks or takes time for pleasure as frivolous or 'selfish'? Shall we start to open our eyes and realise that we're surrounded by sick, exhausted, and upset women instead of sparkly, sassy, sexy ones? Shall we start to question the role of women as the ultimate 'givers' of pleasure and rarely the receivers? We've already seen that the world is set up to suit men and their hormonal cycle, but it's also set up to ensure that men's pleasure and needs are prioritised over women's. For women to not know about the power of their menstrual cycle is damaging and dangerous. It's the same for women to not know or understand the power that pleasure holds for their ultimate health and sparkle.

## Don't Make Me Give That Up!

When I'm seeing clients at my online clinic, a question I often hear is, "You're not going to make me give that up, are you?" – in reference to something they might be telling me about in their diet or lifestyle. No matter what issue a woman comes to me with (be it a skin condition, depression, painful periods, lack of confidence, recurring illness etc), I can always see the sheer terror in her eyes when she discusses the "thing" that's her favourite treat because the thought of giving up a particular food, drink, or activity is often unbearable. Not because she's being stubborn, silly, or lacks willpower but, because this 'thing' is often the only form of pleasure she gets to experience in her daily life.

It's the mum who's run around all day after screaming kids and treasures that large glass of wine after bath time. The woman who always works late and adores the chocolate bar and fizzy drink on the commute home. The woman in a relationship where there's so little intimacy or communication she looks forward to take-aways on the sofa with her partner as a crucial way to connect. The woman who has to budget so tightly in her day to day life that when she clicks on her favourite online shop, she just splurges. I get it. None of these are failings in a woman's character, but usually a cry for and attempt to meet her body and soul's deep need for pleasure.

There's no need to worry, though. I rarely tell a woman she can't keep something in her life – especially when she hasn't yet found another source of pleasure (although, if needs be, I do let her know what the thing might be doing to her body and how it might be contributing to the problem she's sought help with me for). As I explain to my lovely clients, unless you're seriously ill, most of these things *can* be a part of your life. They're just not meant to be your only source of pleasure.

Food, drink, shopping, and hours on social media were never meant to be the quick, easy, and cheap substitutes for the daily, hourly moments of pleasure you should be experiencing as a woman. Once you understand that your female body craves and needs pleasure on a deep level, you'll start to understand that your body may not be deeply and constantly desiring something that causes inflammation, like alcohol or highly processed/sugary foods. It's far more likely it's craving an experience of pleasure and moments of real sweetness that are sorely missing from your day to day life.

For example, if I offered you that glass of wine you think you can't give up or a night in the most beautiful 5-star hotel with no one disturbing you – which would you pick? If I could offer you that packet of biscuits or an hour long full-body massage with essential oils that left you feel completely relaxed – which would you go for? If I could offer you 3 hours on social media or 1 hour with a friend who always makes you laugh and feel amazing – which would you choose? Perhaps you can start to see now that its pleasure your body is constantly asking you for not the "thing" you think you can't do without.

**The Key To Pleasure**

Let me back up my belief that you were designed as a woman to receive and not just give pleasure with some biological facts. Your body has various organs, all of which have a specific purpose to keep you in mental and physical health. No organ exists without a job to do and the better they do that job, the more likely it is that you'll have a happy, healthy, sparkly body. However, there's one organ that I'm guessing you won't have been properly taught about (because if doctors aren't taught in any depth about this organ then neither will you've been). If you don't understand this organ's abilities, needs, and symbolism, then your vitality and sexy sparkle will likely be limited. Only women have this organ and, although it would never be classed as a vital organ by medical professionals, I'm telling you it *is* vital for your happiness, energy, and sexy sparkle. The organ I'm talking about is the clitoris.

I know you'll now think this means that the pleasure I'm going to talk about is sex-based, but it's not. The teachings on the clitoris's function and why it exists have been far too narrow or non-existent. To only think of sex with regard to the clitoris is like only thinking your brain exists to solve math problems. The name 'clitoris' comes from the Greek word for 'key'. If you can start to understand this organ's actual symbolic, sexual *and* non-sexual reasons for being in your body, then I believe you can start to unlock a life filled with more health, joy, and sparkle.

Fact: The clitoris is the *only* organ in the human body (men have no equivalent) that's primary purpose is for you to experience pleasure. *Read that again a few times.*

Do you understand the enormity of what this means for pleasure-starved, exhausted, over-giving women? Pleasure was deemed such a crucial component to your existence that you've been given an organ entirely dedicated to it. Your heart has certain biological functions and it also symbolises your need to give and receive love. In the same way, your clitoris can physically experience pleasure but it also symbolises your female need to not only give, but to consistently receive pleasure.

## Clitoris Facts

- Your clitoris contains at least 8,000 sensory nerve endings. 8,000! To put that into perspective, the penis only has about 4,000! So, you've been given an organ that has the potential to experience double the pleasure of a penis. In a world that champions and often prioritises the pleasure of the penis, remember it's *you* that possesses an organ far more pleasure hungry and sensitive*.

- The clitoris (obviously it varies from woman to woman) is approximately 10cm in length. It's made up of lots of different parts, including the clitoral head, hood, clitoral shaft, urethral sponge, erectile tissue (yes, it's not just the penis that has that), glands, vestibular bulbs and clitoral 'legs'. However, it's only the head and hood (which make up approximately one third of the clitoris) that are outside your body.

- Several major medical textbooks completely leave out the clitoris or simply label it on a diagram but with no further description of it as an organ – unlike the penis which is usually covered in-depth. It wasn't until 1998 that the clitoris was mapped out in its entirety by urologist Helen O'Connell. The lack of knowledge about this organ in a woman's body, and its links to physical and mental health (more of this in a bit), means that once again (like with knowledge about the menstrual cycle) women are missing out on vital health information.

- In the 16th century, it was said that the clitoris didn't appear in 'healthy women' and it was known as the *Devil's Teat*. If a woman was found with one, then she was often deemed to be a witch. By the 1800's, women diagnosed with 'hysteria' sometimes had their clitoris removed – an abhorrent act of violence that still exists today (known as Female Genital Mutilation**) which seeks to inflict pain and deprive women of their God-given right to, and biological need for, pleasure.

- The clitoris actually grows during a woman's lifetime as a result of hormonal changes in the body. By the time a woman is 32, the clitoris will be almost 4 times the size it was at the start of puberty and it often doesn't stop there. This shows you that women's pleasure is meant to *increase* as we get older – not the usual story we hear about women and ageing is it?

- In 2016, the first life-size model of a clitoris was created by the amazing French engineer, researcher, and sociologist Odile Fillod, who realised that seeing what a clitoris looks like (it's beautiful btw) was a vital part of teaching sex education. She wanted to correct the myth that it's 'pea-sized' and that knowledge of women's bodies and pleasure is secondary to men's.

Your clitoris is an internal and external organ, and therefore a reminder that you must take time to find pleasure that satisfies your deep inner needs as well as your more immediate 'outer' ones. The health that pleasure can bring to your body can be both internal (helping to reduce inflammation) and external (making you laugh, smile, or glow).

So, how do you stimulate this powerful organ? Yes, okay, there's the obvious sexual way that everyone associates with the clitoris (*there's more information on this type of 'Cliteracy' at the end of this chapter), but the needs of your female body go way beyond sexual self and partner pleasure. Because there's a fair amount of information out there on sexual pleasure for women, I want us to focus on the non-sexual pleasure info. That's because I think the non-sexual nourishment and pleasure that I see many women missing out on is a foundational component to their sexual pleasure (and pleasure of their whole lives), but it's not much talked about.

Ever wondered why sometimes when women eat certain foods or buy certain items they refer to them as 'orgasmic' or 'better than sex'? It's because they're tuned in to their clitoris and its "language" and need for pleasure. It's time to get rid of the narrow choices of female pleasure we've been given – generally food, shopping, wine and sex – and reclaim the full depth and breadth of the pleasures we were always meant to enjoy in this life. We want to get back to our bodies and minds experiencing singing, dancing, belly-laughing, napping, swimming, being silly, being pampered, not being busy, being with our most favourite people and savouring not scoffing our most favourite food and drinks – because we know it's *all* allowed, needed and deeply nourishing.

We want to be women who are fully (or at least partially for now if that seems too big a leap) 'turned on' by our lives. We want to reclaim our clitoris, seek out moments (however fleeting or long) of pleasure so we're 'aroused' by something on a daily basis that has nothing to do with sex (but can of course include it). It's this glow, spring in your step, and sparkle in your eyes that would only normally be associated with a woman experiencing lots of great sex with a new lover. This is to become the norm for you and your life – with or without that lover!

**Superpower Sparkle Gas**

Pleasure isn't just something "nice" for women to have if they're able to get it. It's actual medicine and should be prescribed as readily as the other medications women are often given. This is because when you experience pleasure, a wonderful chemical compound called Nitric Oxide is released into your body. Nitric Oxide, or as I like to call it your 'Superpower Sparkle Gas', has immense health and sexy sparkle boosting properties. It's produced by the cells that line your blood vessels and its discovery for health was so important it even won a Nobel Prize.

When you experience or even just think about something pleasurable, your Superpower Sparkle Gas (Nitric Oxide) is released in your body. Here are just some of the magical benefits your body, mind, and sexy sparkle can get from it:

- It can help your *whole body* function better by improving your circulation.
- It can help balance all of your other 'feel-good' hormones (the same ones many women are prescribed medication for when they feel low or depressed).
- It can help reset negative thinking/behaviours, allowing new neural pathways to form in your brain.
- It works to help your body fight infections, reduce inflammation, and even destroy tumours.
- It can help to reduce blood pressure.
- It can help protect against dementia.

- It's the chemical that *actually lights the glow of a firefly*, so think how much it could relight your sexy sparkle and glow!

Can you see why I think your Superpower Sparkle Gas that gets released daily or hourly by moments of pleasure should be being prescribed to all women as well as (or before) various medications? Perhaps when some of us are feeling low, anxious, or depressed, part of the issue is that we don't have enough pleasure or Nitric Oxide in our lives and bodies.

If you feel exhausted at the thought of trying to do something pleasurable or it feels too unobtainable or unachievable for you right now, it's important to remember that your body makes no distinction between *thinking* about something and actually *doing* it. For example, stress hormones are still released into your body whether you're thinking about something terrible happening or it actually happening. It's the same for your Superpower Sparkle Gas – Nitric Oxide can be released simply by you choosing to think about pleasurable things or experiences. Shut your eyes and think of something right now that you find pleasurable... congratulations, you just gave your health a boost from your Superpower Sparkle Gas.

Here's some activities that can release your Superpower Sparkle Gas:

- Belly-laughing.
- Being in the sunshine.
- Having a massage.
- Savouring your favourite food or drink.
- Moving your body – everything from a run, gentle swim, walk in nature, or just cartwheeling barefoot across the grass.
- Breathing deeply through your nose.
- Being grateful for something.
- Meditating.
- Having an orgasm.
- Thinking about any of the above or anything else you find pleasurable.

I think it's so exciting there's an actual health and sparkle-boosting superpower that's free and can be activated whenever you like. Increased amounts of pleasure, fun, and joy in your life can actually positively impact your hormones, too. When we think of our hormones, we usually think of the sex hormones oestrogen, progesterone, and testosterone. However, we should always pay attention to DHEA because it's known as the 'master-hormone' and creates all of our sex hormones. DHEA levels increase when we experience pleasure, joy, and happiness and this in turn balances our oestrogen, progesterone, and testosterone which boosts our overall health and vitality. Can you see how important it is?

A way to boost your levels of your Superpower Sparkle Gas is by eating foods that are high in nitrates such as gorgeous greens like kale, spinach, rocket etc, and foods with high levels of antioxidants like walnuts, garlic, berries, broccoli, blueberries, and dark chocolate. Beetroot is also brilliant for helping fuel your production of Nitric Oxide, as are hemp seeds – so get adding them to your soups, salads, stews or pop them in your smoothies.

## Enemies Of Your Superpower Sparkle Gas

If you're not feeling the sparkle-boosting benefits of your Superpower Sparkle Gas when you're already going to yoga, sipping your favourite drink, orgasming, or thinking about pleasurable things, you're most likely being affected by enemies of your Superpower Sparkle Gas.

It may not come as much surprise that some of the biggest enemies of your energy, hormonal balance, and overall health also deplete or suppress your Nitric Oxide levels:

- chronic inflammation
- toxins in your food and environment
- not eating enough gorgeous greens

- not doing enough marvellous movement
- emotional stress

Let's have a quick chat about emotional stress because it's a biggie for women. Women are natural problem solvers and desire to help others, but can be deeply affected not only by the pain and struggle of those they know, but also the problems in the world. The 24-hour stream of global bad news from the media is super toxic to your health and sparkle. You have to take some moments to know you were never meant to shoulder *all* the hurts of this world and deny yourself pleasure just because someone else is in pain. You don't stop drinking clean water just because someone else doesn't have access to it (although you can certainly help others get these vital things, too). Don't do the same with pleasure – don't deny yourself it (and the health it can bring you and those around you) because you can't ensure everyone is having it.

Originally, you would've lived in a tribe and only had to know about the issues of your immediate communities – where there would've been a balance of good as well as not so good things happening. In that environment, you would've had the ability to help others who were struggling, whilst still being acutely aware of and experiencing all the joy and pleasure that was around you. Feeling constantly sad and helpless by world events (not that we shouldn't be informed and of course get involved with causes we're passionate about) or others' lives can deplete your own health and sparkle.

We all, of course, experience and have to deal with times of extreme stress, grief, and worry. However, this was never meant to be your permanent or normal state of being. You were always meant to move past these times of pain and struggle, and move back into times of daily pleasure, joy, health, and sparkle. You have a right to pleasure, so take a break from the heavy burdens that watching the mainstream media can bring. Try to remember all the people you know and love who aren't suffering right now. This can help bring some sparkle where before there was only stress and feeling like there was pain and struggle all around.

## Daily Pleasure Practices

Your clitoris represents your biological need for pleasure, and your Superpower Sparkle Gas (Nitric Oxide) provides the health benefits of pleasure. So, how do you get this power couple working in perfect harmony? Well, just as one sit-up won't give you a 6-pack, a frenzied stuffing of biscuits or downing of wine you love won't give you the deep holistic pleasure your body needs. What you need is daily (or even better, hourly) moments of true, acknowledged, unadulterated pleasure. Sound excessive? Well, if you don't think it's excessive that your heart beats around 4800 times an hour or you take 12-20 breaths a minute, then your clitoris needing a few moments of pleasure each day is certainly not over the top in the demanding organ stakes.

It's time to start cultivating your 'Daily Pleasure Practices' so it feels effortless and not something else for you to try and remember to do.

**Here's Some Of My Daily Or Weekly Pleasure Practices That Boost My Sexy Sparkle:**

- I walk my dog and love watching her set her own pace and not be hurried by others.

- I get out in nature.

- I make my morning matcha or green tea as if I'm making it for royalty. I treat myself to the finest tea my budget allows, I brew it in a beautiful cup, and I make sure the first 2 or 3 sips are taken as if they're the very elixir of life. I know for many of you, your morning may start by tearing around after your kids or rushing to work. However, could you have this moment of pleasure before they get up or when they're at school or taking a nap? Could you get to work earlier or stop off on the way and grab your favourite drink from somewhere so there's a moment of acknowledged pleasure in your day before the busyness begins?

■ If I want chocolate, instead of a cheap, crappy bar inhaled right there and then (which used to be my habit), I'll now try and wait until I have at least 30 minutes in my day to enjoy it so that any inflammation that the sugar may cause in my body is balanced out by an experience of deep, nourishing pleasure. I take some time (as my friend Tamu Thomas from LiveThreeSixty.com would say) to "romance myself". I've realised I don't need to rely on others for romance and pleasure (and certainly not chocolates or flowers), I can bring those things into my life myself.

This is how I try and have chocolate at least once a week if I'm craving a sugary treat (WARNING – this may be too pleasurably explicit for you!): I run myself a bath with Epsom salts and frankincense oil. I pour myself a glass of sparkling kombucha. I arrange 4 of my favourite truffles (decadent, hazelnut truffles from Booja Booja if you must know) on the prettiest plate I have and take it to the bathroom with my kombucha. I sink into the bath, take a big inhale through my nose, and exhale through my mouth and feel every single one of my muscles relax. Then, once I'm relaxed, I treat myself to my first truffle. I use all of my senses, marveling at the smell, sight, and texture of the chocolate. Once I'm focused on how pleasurable this moment is, how much my body has been crying out for it, I then take a slow and sultry bite of this sweet treat, acknowledge my clitoris and know my Superpower Sparkle Gas has been released throughout my body. Now how sexy is that? You see sexiness and self-pleasure can be fully experienced, but doesn't need to involve physical sex at all if you don't want it to.

All that took was 30 minutes of my time to reap the physical and emotional rewards of a pleasure practice that previously would've simply involved me angrily eating a packet of chocolate biscuits in my kitchen as I made dinner. The worst thing you can do is have food or drinks that are stressful to your body and cause inflammation (sugar, alcohol, highly processed foods, etc) and then not take a moment to acknowledge your clitoris and have them as a mentally and physically pleasurable experience (to reduce the inflammation).

If you're someone who literally can't find 15-30 minutes in your day to pleasure yourself and take time to enjoy a specific food, drink or experience that you love, then could you take your favourite treat and just go sit in your bedroom, car or outside for just 5 minutes, breathe in deeply through your nose, engage your senses, acknowledge

226

your clitoris, and enjoy your moment of pleasure, no matter how brief it is?

- I've stopped regularly eating dinner on my lap in front of the TV because I don't enjoy it and can find it stressful (especially if the news is on). The reason I used to do this was because that's how my husband gains pleasure. Dinner in front of the TV, especially when the football is on, is utter bliss to him. However, it's the opposite for me. So, one day I realised that this wasn't a needed element in our relationship. I realised that I could sit at the kitchen table, eat and savour my food with my favourite radio station on or in silence instead of being hunched over a plate on the sofa, seething that the football was on again.

  This was so damaging to my mind, body, and our relationship. There's nothing sad or worrying in our relationship if we don't always eat dinner together every night, just the understanding that we both deserve pleasure and don't need to always compromise. Is there a daily compromise you make with a loved one that ends up not satisfying either of you and stealing your pleasure, health and sparkle too?

- My final pleasure practice in my day is before I get into bed, I try and take a deep inhale of my favourite essential oil (frankincense) and then sprinkle some of my pillow before I lie down. This brings me my final acknowledged moment of pleasure as I end my day.

## Over To You

I know you want to look after others and bring them happiness, joy, and pleasure – I do, too. However, this should always come from a place of you being full of health and pleasure first. There are always opportunities to fit more macro or mini moments of pleasure into your day, so start looking for them. Think of at least two things that you could do in your current daily life that would boost your pleasure factor from 1 to 8,000 (remember this is the approximate number of pleasure endings in your clitoris).

- Could you have your morning drink out of a nicer cup or in a dressing gown that makes you feel fabulous not frumpy?
- Could you buy yourself a wonderful shower gel that you love the smell of (instead of just buying the cheapest) or put some drops of essential oil in your current shower gel to transport your body and mind to your favourite holiday or spa destination? I was told the other day that if you hang fresh eucalyptus branches (with the leaves) in your shower then the steam helps to release its invigorating fragrance.

Now, that does sound like a good way to increase the pleasure of your shower.

- Could you eat your meals in a more pleasurable way, on a nicer plate, with nicer cutlery or include more foods that make *you* feel fabulous (or have more nitrates in them to boost your Superpower Sparkle Gas)?

- Could you decide that for five minutes every day, you'll lie on your bed, breathe deeply in and out through your nose (this is thought to help reset your nervous system), and say good things about yourself, your day, and your life?

- Could you call someone who makes you laugh as opposed to stresses you out?

- Could you savour the foods/drinks you love (especially if they're not fabulous for your health) so that your body isn't having them *and* feeling stressed?

- Could you go for a walk in a place you truly love and take a moment to appreciate it?

- Could you play a song you love and dance to it once a day?

- What is a bedtime ritual you could start that would add one final pop of pleasure to your day?

You get the idea….

Of course, let's not forget pleasure can also be bought. So, if you have the money, then honey, you GO FOR IT! Get every spa treatment, dinner out, holiday, and trinket that gets your pleasure points pulsating and your Superpower Sparkle Gas flowing. However, you can hopefully also see that pleasure doesn't need to be bought and isn't just for rich women. It's for every woman to pursue and experience in her daily life.

Looking after yourself and making time for pleasure might feel so uncomfortable and selfish, but you *have* to just get over it. Being selfless means you're *less* than yourself. I don't want you to be *less* than yourself, I want you to be and have *more!* I want you to have more health, vitality, pleasure, and Sexy Sparkle. So, let's stop criticising the women who look after themselves and pursue pleasure. Let's stop championing the women who 'never stop'. Let's stop thinking that the best obituary a woman can have is one that says "she always put everyone else first", because I've seen this written too many times about women who've died young and known in my gut that these two things could be related.

It's a courageous act to say goodbye to guilt, disease, depression, anger, resentment, being a martyr, and always being exhausted. It takes guts to stand up as a woman and announce that pleasure is *your divine right* and embedded *in your divine design*. When a man exudes confidence and has a swagger that announces, "I'm something special," he's often described as having 'Big Dick Energy'. Well, I want us women to start having a sparkle in our eyes, a spring in our step, a body so filled-up with pleasure (and the health that brings) that we're described as having 'Big Clit Energy'.

**Just one quick piece of advice on your libido**
**before I wrap up this chapter...**
**...focus on your VPA not your VPL.**

Many women's feelings of sexiness and their libido can dwindle as the years pass. The common explanation given to women is usually "it's your age" or "it's your hormones" or both. This is once again sticking to the boring and incorrect narrative that women's fun, happiness, health, sexiness, and sparkle is always reduced with age. Along with the idea that their pesky, flawed, and dwindling hormones means their fertility, libido, potential and presence in this world is drying up. Well I call BS! Yes, some women may want or need some support through supplements, synthetic or bio-identical hormones or pharmaceuticals if they feel their sex drive drop and are unhappy about it – but, these shouldn't be dished out and devoured without addressing the other sparkle suppressing elements in a woman's life. Like not having enough pleasure to be turned on by her own life, let alone a partner.

Not seeking or experiencing pleasure in your day to day life affects your ability to feel turned on emotionally, spiritually as well as physically and they're all deeply connected. Yes, of course inflammation, hormonal shifts/imbalances, or other health problems can affect a woman's sex drive but, it can also be from the fact women have been taught to focus more on the type of sexiness linked with a VPL instead of their VPA.

Now, I was a teenager and in my early twenties at a time where thongs were heralded as the sexiest, most fashion-friendly type of underwear for women. Why? Well, because it meant when you wore tight clothes (which are again presented as one of the sexiest types of clothes you can wear for men's visual pleasure as opposed to your comfort and pleasure) a thong prevents you from having a VPL or 'Visible Panty Line'. No VPL gives the illusion that you have no underwear on and therefore makes a woman's tight clothing even more titillating to the male gaze (which women in my generation have been unconsciously trained to dress for – this is thankfully starting to change!).

I was taught as a young woman by the media and celebrities which underwear, namely thongs (or as I now like to think of them – uncomfortable, bacteria-spreading, bum floss) meant I wouldn't have a VPL, meaning my outfit and me could appear more sexy and attractive. I now know I should've been being taught about my VPA and what makes *me* feel more sexy or attractive in my own body, not the things I should do/not do to increase the pleasure of others when they view me.

Now a woman's VPA – 'Vaginal Pulse Amplitude' (also known as the 'hidden heartbeat') – is the amount of blood flow in her vaginal walls when she's aroused and turned on. This is a common way to measure a woman's libido if she's having problems in this area (using a vaginal photometer if you're interested). Your VPA will also change throughout your menstrual cycle and different seasons of life.

What I've found is that most studies done on what increases the VPA of women were carried out in the same way as studies on men's arousal – normally showing an erotic video, an anxiety-inducing video and a 'neutral' video then seeing the difference in the body's responses. But, as we've learnt, women's bodies, minds and pleasure practices are usually completely different to men and a more female-focused study showed that women's VPA wasn't increased substantially by looking at pictures of muscly firemen; thinking about getting dressed up in lingerie, tight clothes, or adhering to the "traditional" male ideas of sexiness. No, the things that really saw a women's VPA (and therefore libido/feelings of being 'turned on') skyrocket were:

a) Feeling protected and safe

b) Experiencing or being surrounded by beauty, nature, or creativity
c) Being/feeling adored

I think these results will surprise men, but not women. It's why many women can get more 'turned on' or find pleasure in watching a romantic drama or comedy where a woman is being adored or protected by a partner or suitor, more than a graphic sexual scene or story (not saying women don't find this arousing too though).

It makes me frustrated that women are being told their dwindling hormones, need for synthetic drugs, ageing bodies etc. are all reasons they don't feel turned on and desire sex like they used to. They're often told to address these "problems" in a very male way eg. buy sexy clothes, make time for sex, take some medication (and if all/any of those things help or appeal to you, then of course you should feel empowered to use them). However, far more likely for the reduction in women's libido is that along with too much inflammation in their bodies, women are not pursuing, feeling, or thinking they deserve pleasure. They're not spending enough time in nature, tapping into their creative side, or experiencing any true beauty in their lives. A reduction in confidence (don't worry, we'll work on this in the 'Secret of Your Sparkle' chapter) or change in circumstances can mean women don't feel protected and safe in themselves, lives or a relationship. Plus, a belief that you're not allowed to ask for the things you want and should just be happy with your lot in life, means that many women live feeling put upon instead of being or feeling adored (by themselves or a partner).

So, any client of mine who's struggling with not feeling sexy, turned on by her life and has a flagging libido, I don't tell her that her first option is to start taking extra hormones or medication. I ask her to first infuse pleasure into her daily life. To experience more beauty. To get out in nature more. To take up or restart a creative pursuit. And to ask herself if she feels (by herself first and then her significant partner if she has one) safe, protected and adored? These are the things that'll increase a woman's Sexy Sparkle and can be started to be addressed right away.

So, go and say a big 'yes' to yourself and your desires, and let other women be astounded and admire you. You don't need permission for pleasure. Pleasure is key to your vitality, ongoing health, and getting your sparkle back. Pursue it, enjoy it, and infuse it into your hours and days. Your Sexy Sparkle isn't an aim, it's the natural energy and attitude of a woman who seeks, allows, and adores pleasure to be part of her life once more.

## 2 Small Sparkly Steps For Today...

1) I want you to go grab a food or drink that brings you true pleasure. Now close your eyes and think of someone you really, really love. Breathe in deeply and feel the love you have for them expand and fill your physical heart. Breathe out knowing the health of your heart and whole body has been improved from this thinking, acknowledging and experience of love.

   Okay, open your eyes. Now I want you to slowly eat or drink your chosen item and, in the same way you experienced the feeling of love in your heart without touching it, I want you to focus on and experience the feeling of pleasure in your clitoris (it may feel similar to doing a pelvic floor exercise) without touching it.

   Revel in the taste and texture of your food or drink, let the feelings of pleasure travel up from your clitoris and fill your whole body knowing that this pleasure is bringing your health and life a boost. Now, imagine Superpower Sparkle Gas being released throughout your body like a cascade of glitter and light, lighting you up from head to toe (just as it does that firefly). I want you to understand that when you experience physical pleasure like this, it's also spiritual. There's no shame in pleasure (the opposite of what many religions have taught), it was created by God to increase your light and health. Remember acknowledging and engaging your heart in any feelings of true, deep love only amplifies the experience for you. The same is true if you acknowledge and engage your clitoris when having moments, no matter how brief, of pleasure.

2) This week I want you to increase your VPA by finding a way to either spend more time in nature, pursue a creative hobby/task or increase the beauty of your surroundings. Take a picture of you doing this as a reminder that you'll feel more turned on and tuned into your body when you feel more turned on by your life.

*Cliteracy* – *As much as the clitoris has a role in and represents our need for pleasure, there's obviously its physical ability to bring sexual pleasure. Go check out the amazing resource that is 'Cliteracy' by Sophia Wallace, to learn more about the history, anatomy and role in sex of this unique and special organ http://projects.huffingtonpost.com/projects/cliteracy*

**Female Genital Mutilation** – *I'm no specialist and don't have a sound base of knowledge in the area of FGM, so that's why I'm not expanding on this subject at length. However, after learning more about how vital pleasure and our clitoris is, I do know that for a practice to* *exist that removes it from a woman's body to try and eradicate her pleasure (be that sexual or of life in general) is barbaric. If you're in the UK and have been affected by this issue or know anyone who has, please go to https://www.dofeve.org/?s=FGM where further resources and help can be found, or speak to your GP. Also please know that, yes, your clitoris is a physical organ, but the clitoris is representative of your right as a woman to experience pleasure. If for any reason you don't have a clitoris, you're still created and able to experience pleasure, because it's not reliant on you having a clitoris.*

# SPEAK UP FOR YOUR SPARKLE

If I'd have written this book seven years ago, this chapter wouldn't have been included because I hadn't yet made or experienced the connection between the importance of women speaking up for themselves and their sparkle. However, after experiencing mental and physical health problems due to not being able to truly express myself and my needs to others, I now know what you're about to read is vital to you having your best health and getting your sparkle back.

I've never had a problem with talking. I'm a really good talker. I'm the person who chats to people at bus stops, in the supermarket, or when I'm walking the dog. I'm the person who gets put next to quiet people at weddings so the conversation keeps flowing. I know how to fill awkward silences and put people at ease and I like doing it. If you know me, you'd probably describe me as talkative and confident. You'd never think that I've had *real* problems speaking up for myself.

What I've discovered, however, is that talking and speaking up for yourself are entirely different things. Talking is generally easy, encouraged, and seen as a normal thing for women to do – we're caricatured as "chatterboxes", gossips, and nags. But, speaking up, oh no, that's traditionally been seen as naturally more of a man's domain – hence why most politicians, CEOs, and other types of leaders are still men. For women, speaking up is actually often considered confrontational, unladylike, and a negative trait. But, for men it's seen as a sign of power, confidence, and success (yawn).

From a young age, "no one likes a tell-tale" or "don't be so bossy" are common chastisements given to little girls who express their displeasure or annoyance of another person or situation or speak up for what they want. This then progresses into women who speak up for themselves being labelled again as "bossy", "outspoken", or "ball-breakers". So, if being outspoken isn't championed for women, where does that leave us? Often, it means many women remain "unspoken", or even worse, "in-spoken", a situation where imaginary conversations or expressions of anger or standing up for themselves happen only inside their head.

Keeping your feelings inside shouldn't be praised as virtuous, peace-keeping, kind and feminine because it's actually super damaging to your health and sparkle. But, not speaking up for yourself has become so normalised for many women that they even find it easier to have sex with a person or partner than share their true feelings with them – don't you think that's kind of wrong? Don't you think we should've been taught how valuable it was for us to speak up and believe it's as needed and desired for us to share our thoughts and feelings as it is our time and bodies? If talk is cheap, then speaking up for yourself as a woman is pure, sparkling gold – and it's more of that gold I want in your life.

## A Good Woman

As children, we quickly discover the ways to gain love and approval, and also how to lose it. No child wants to disappoint their parents, teachers, or authority figures, and so as little girls, many of us stopped speaking up because we realised that it could displease or disrupt the happiness of those we loved or wanted to please. We worked out that "good" little girls don't moan, shout, or scream about how they're feeling because silence, holding back, and having controlled emotions are more often applauded. Whereas anger, rage, and snot-ridden tears are often seen as dramatic, diva-ish, demanding, and are tried to be stopped whenever they appear.

"Good" women are meant to keep the status quo and not rock the boat – at home, at work, or in relationships. "Good" women are meant to just bottle things up so they don't offend others, make a scene, or make others uncomfortable. We're taught time and time again from a young age that being overly emotional simply makes us seem unstable and even unreliable as women. We get the message that "easy going women" who don't make a fuss, demand things or constantly speak up for themselves are the most desirable ones.

The thing is, I don't want you to be a "good" woman or be seen as "easy going" to potential or current partners (which is something I strove to be for years and silenced my true self and sparkle). I want you to shake off a history where women were demonised for speaking up for their own or others' needs, or speaking out against religious, medical, or political institutions that regularly took away their rights. I use the word 'demonised' deliberately because one of the ways women could avoid being tried, tortured, and killed during the 16th century (and beyond) witch trials, was to "...blend in and *not* to seem too openly self-assertive. To be, or to behave, otherwise was to open oneself to suspicion of witchcraft..." (from the book *Witches, Midwives and Nurses* by Barabara Ehernreich and Deirdre English). An assertive woman (along with nurses and midwives) may no longer be in danger of being called or burnt as a witch, but can subtly be outcast in other ways.

You're allowed to ask questions. You're allowed to be a "trouble-maker". You're allowed to make things awkward by not just going along with what you've been asked to. You're allowed to have opinions that aren't those of the majority. You're allowed to make a fuss and disagree with people in power. You're allowed to just say you're over the way your life has been going and want things to change. I don't want you to be unspoken and in-spoken and leave all your thoughts, concerns, and questions inside of your mind where they can torment you. Your headache shouldn't be easier to talk about than your heartache. I want you to freely and effortlessly speak up about what you're *truly* feeling.

I want you to find it easy to speak up about what's hurting you, what rocks your world, what's exhausting you, what's worrying you, what you're outraged about, what you dream of doing (but feel too silly to say out loud), and even what you *really* just want for dinner. I want you to be able to speak up without constantly worrying about or putting others' needs first. This isn't so you become self-absorbed. It's to help you become the sassy, sexy, vibrant, confident, joyful, rebellious, dream-chasing, world-changing, outspoken woman with sparkle you were created to be. This version of you may not keep those around you as happy but, it's *this* version of you that the world needs more of. I want you to have the health, happiness, and life you deserve. That can't truly start without you speaking up for yourself.

**Just to say…**

It's important to differentiate between speaking up and moaning. Speaking up isn't about constantly making yourself a victim or martyr in any given situation (which can be done through both speaking or staying silent) as that's draining for everyone around you and will do nothing for your sparkle. Of course, we all like to vent about our jobs, partners, and bad days, but speaking up is different.

The key to speaking up is having an objective. It's about voicing your issues with an aim to finding a solution that'll increase your health and sparkle. Speaking up is the first important step to making needed and positive changes in your life. Whereas moaning is just dead-end complaining and negativity. So, don't simply moan to your partner or other people about a crappy situation and expect anything to be different. Speak up and confidently explain how you feel and what help you need from them to enable you to reach a sparkle-filled solution.

## What does speaking up for yourself mean?

- It's being able to express a desire, no matter how big or small, without constantly worrying what others will think of you.

- It's not needing permission from anyone before you express your true feelings.

- It's having an equal voice in relationships – whether that's with friends, colleagues, your partner, or family.

- It's being able to clearly express your needs on a daily basis and explain how you'd like others to help or support you (it doesn't mean they will, but that's not in your control).

- It's about not thinking others – regardless of their profession, financial status, or family relationship to you – cannot be questioned, disagreed with, scrutinized, or asked about their behavior, opinion, or actions.

- It's about being free.

**What speaking up for yourself doesn't mean?**

- It doesn't mean you think other voices are less important than yours.

- It doesn't mean you don't allow others to speak up and be heard.

- It doesn't mean that you use "speaking your truth" as a weapon to hurt, gossip or belittle innocent people.

**E-motion**

When 'silent killers' are talked about, it's normally in reference to a physical disease that you may not know you have until it's too late. In my opinion, silence itself is a killer. I'm not talking about the stillness and golden silence that's part of rest, prayer, and meditation (which by the way, is super important for your sparkle). I'm talking about the silent hurts, traumas, tough times, frustrations, hopes and dreams that you've stuffed deep down inside of you and are unable to express. It's *that* silence that can be killing your sparkle and hurting your soul. You were never meant to hold so much inside and ignore your emotions. You were never meant to constantly push down your feelings for fear of upsetting, offending, or displeasing people. You were never meant to exist as a version of yourself to please others, but disappoint yourself.

I believe that the 'e' in emotion stands for energy. Emotion therefore is basically 'energy-in-motion' and it's meant to move through you and not be stuck. You're meant to feel your emotions, speak about them, work through them, and move them out of your body. Your emotions aren't a mistake or nuisance you need to try and neutralise. They contain wisdom to help you express the truth of who you are. Yes, some emotions are like clouds and can be fleeting, but I'm talking about the deep emotions you feel that if you had no fear you'd express. Emotion was never meant to just fester inside your body for days, weeks, or years and create a form of decay.

Trapped emotions can cause all sorts of mental and physical problems – everything from weariness that you can't explain, IBS, skin problems, anxiety, and many more serious symptoms that prevent you from living your best, most sparkly life. Don't let the description of being "emotional" or "overly-emotional" be a way of shaming you or another woman who expresses herself.

Your emotions are a powerful form of health and energy that should never be seen as negative. Don't ignore them. Listen to them. What are they trying to teach you or alert you to? How are they trying to bring balance and happiness to your body and your life? What are they trying to express or release and move out of your body? What are they trying to direct you away from and towards? How are they trying to lead you back to your sparkle? Remember, if the word "motion" is in emotion, it's meant to move.

## Depression Or Suppression?

Many women struggle with feelings of anxiety and depression. The reasons vary from person to person and can be multi-faceted, but in my professional and personal experience, the feelings of depression can often be because of the suppression of feelings. Women have a habit of not expressing their emotions and pushing down their true feelings. Most women are suppressing them, sometimes to the point they aren't even aware of them (i.e. repressing them), because often they can feel too big or sometimes too trivial and unimportant to be aired.

Many women are walking around unable to express their true feelings of anger, rage, annoyance, loneliness, exhaustion, frustration, sadness, boredom, fear, and grief because they've learnt that a "good" woman who doesn't cause problems for others hides, not expresses their feelings. So often when I speak to a client and ask them why they get teary, moody, or angry just before or during their period, they can't tell me. They just palm it off as "hormones" or try and joke about their own mental instability – which funnily enough (or not as the case may be) are how many men dismiss women's emotions being expressed.

However, these symptoms of anger or tears are often your body's inability to keep suppressing the things that feel depressing to you. Your body knows that you're fed up of being ignored by your partner; or undermined by a parent; underpaid by your job; exhausted by your children; bored of having to cook; fearful about a loved one's health; sad about an incident that happened a month ago; angry with your selfish friend; plagued by thoughts of the past; frustrated with not feeling happy in yourself or living the life you want to be. Your body knows the truth that you're refusing to acknowledge or are unable to express, and when your hormone and energy levels drop before and during your period, those suppressed emotions tend to rise to the surface (they also do this again in the Sparkly Shift of the Perimenopause). Because you've spent the previous weeks or months, or years ignoring them, you often don't know (or are afraid to admit) where the tears, anger, or sadness is coming from. So, most women accept the labels of "hormonal" or "crazy" and even give them to their selves.

When women's feelings are constantly edited by others and the world in general, then emotions are constantly suppressed. They then can become repressed, often leaving a woman having no idea why she's feeling depressed. We don't allow women to regularly feel and express the emotions they need to, mainly because it's inconvenient in keeping the 24-hour male-centred working world ticking along as it's been set up to. So, women get taught which emotions they can or *should* feel or express openly, and which they most definitely shouldn't in case (shock horror) they make someone else uncomfortable, upset or have to do something for them.

For instance, if a woman has had a miscarriage, she's often urged to feel happy that she already has a child or is alive herself. If a woman is wanting more from a relationship, she's told she should feel lucky she's not single. If a woman has struggled with her journey/treatment of cancer, she's told she should feel lucky that she's alive. If a woman is struggling with the demands of a newborn or her children, she's told she should be grateful she has children. If a woman's bored, frustrated, angry, and rightly full of rage about something, she's told she should just focus on the positive, profess overall gratitude, and move on.

This constant gaslighting of women's emotions and banning of any perceived negative, wild, or uncontrolled emotion has forced women to suppress the range of true and healthy feelings which they should be allowed to express. I believe this can then lead to some women feeling or being diagnosed with depression. It's taken "thinking positively" to the extreme of becoming very toxic for women who think this is what they should do and feel all the time.

I've experienced various times in my life when I was shouting and screaming inside my head instead of out my mouth. Times when I suppressed huge emotions to the point I didn't even know they were there anymore, and these repressed emotions have always then made me feel utterly depressed. I've felt unable to speak out to ex-bosses or boyfriends or family members about how I was really feeling, and it just made me lose more of my true self and sparkle. Many clients tell me they feel depressed or have been diagnosed with depression and one the first things we do (if it's safe for the client to do that because it's not trauma based) is see if it's because of things that they want to say that have been or are being suppressed.

Before you allow yourself to be labelled (sometimes for life) with a diagnosis of depression, put your hand on your heart and ask your body, "What emotions are you suppressing right now? What is it you want to speak up about but feel unable to?" It's always helpful to get a recommended professional to help guide you through this process if needed.

Suppression in medicine is when a discharge or secretion is stopped from coming out of the body. Discharge and secretions are the body's way of expelling things that need to be moved out of the body so it can stay in health. Suppressing them for a long time would cause all sorts of problems including dangerous infections. It's the same with your mind and feelings – if you constantly suppress the "secretions" that your mind is asking you to expel (anger, fear, rage, helplessness, loneliness, feeling lost, exhaustion etc) by pushing down your emotions and not speaking up, it can lead to all sorts of problems from mild unhappiness to serious depression. Make sure any treatment you undertake for being depressed or feeling anxious includes helping you work through emotions that you could be suppressing. The truth of how you are feeling must come up and out.

## A Snuffed-Out Sparkle

The first time I made the direct link between my suppressed emotions and the physical effect they were having on my body was when I moved overseas for my husband's job. I initially handled the move well. I had fun, made a few friends, and felt proud that I'd helped my husband pursue his dream career. I felt like I was being a "good wife". However, when his job ended sooner than expected, we quickly moved again and I didn't do so well. I really, *really* struggled. The process of trying to make a new life all over again was too much for me. I had no friends, hadn't learnt the language like I'd hoped I would, couldn't get any regular work, was constantly stressed at our precarious financial situation, felt like I had no purpose, and was desperately lonely.

I didn't know how to speak up about how I truly felt because I'd only ever seen women hide how they felt or "crack on" during tough times so as not to worry anyone. So, I pretended that I was "fine". I didn't understand how a simple change in circumstances could take me from being confident, seemingly assertive, and enjoying my sparkle, to becoming insecure, nervous, anxious, and having my sparkle snuffed out. I just couldn't bring myself to speak up about how desperately sad I felt because I didn't want to disappoint my husband, worry others, or admit that perhaps I'd failed to make this new and seemingly great opportunity work.

I suppressed my true emotions for so long that my body started to give me warning signals (just like it had done years earlier with my hormonal imbalance) through physical symptoms. The mind and body are linked (well they're actually one, but it's often easier to talk about them separately). If you're not speaking up for yourself and moving those big emotions through and out of your body, your body will often tell you there's a problem by giving you a mental and/or physical symptom. Suppressed emotion is highly stressful to your body and can cause inflammation. It's that pesky inflammation that we don't want to leave unchecked so that it becomes chronic and causes a variety of mild or serious health problems.

The way the inflammation, caused by the stress of my suppressed emotions, began showing up in my body was through eczema. First, on my wrists and hands, and then progressively it got worse until my whole body (except for my face) became covered in painful, horrible looking eczema. My body was trying to physically get my attention, show me that all was not well, and begging me to make a change. However, I didn't make the connection between my silent sadness and stress of my suppressed emotions and my external physical pain for a long time.

My diet was nutritionally near-perfect and I exercised most days. I saw top doctors, skin specialists, tried Chinese medicine, and anything else that I was recommended. I used the gentlest, most natural products and treatments on my skin, and when those didn't work, I used the strongest, harshest pharmaceuticals. Nothing worked! I spent my days crying with feelings of hopelessness and my nights awake in pain from my burning, cracking skin. I was in deep, dark physical and mental pain but I kept trying to just deal with the problem externally and superficially. I didn't take my own advice and get to the root cause because I didn't know how to speak up about my unhappiness.

For 18 months, I struggled. When my husband got home from work every day and asked how I was – do you know what I'd say? "Oh, I'm fine." Fine! Inside I'd be screaming, "I hate it here. I'm in so much pain! I'm so lonely! I cry every single day! I'm exhausted from not sleeping! I'm scared this is my life now! I feel so down and depressed! I'm so angry you've not noticed all of this. I can't go on like this." But, without fail, I'd normally fake smile and say, "I'm fine," then ask about his day and talk about dinner.

How many times have you been filled with anger, rage, sadness, exhaustion, desperation, loneliness, and pain and instead of speaking up and moving that emotion through your body and asking someone you love and trust to hear and help you, you picked the one phrase we women know all too well: "I'm fine." We have to stop lying about how we're truly feeling. You're worth speaking up for. If you'd speak up for a suffering, sad, or struggling child, then you must speak up for yourself too because you're just as precious.

My daily declarations that I was "fine" seems utter madness now. At the time I felt selfish. I felt that I could only really speak up for myself if I had the solution (either practical, financial, or professional) that could improve our situation, and I didn't. I didn't think it was fair to bring a huge problem of "I hate my life" to my husband, who was working hard and dealing with his own stuff, without having the magic wand to fix it all, either. So, I carried on struggling and suffering, and so did my skin.

However, after 18 months of my fake "fines", I broke down. I sobbed, I raged, I wrote letter after letter to my husband to try and explain how I felt because I couldn't express myself properly in normal conversations. I started to move that suppressed emotion out of my depressed and diseased body (i.e. not at ease body. You must know, there's a connection between dis-ease and disease) and was finally honest about how I was feeling. I spoke up for myself instead of waiting for my husband to gain the skill of telepathy that I believed he should have developed on our wedding day.

From the moment I started speaking up for myself, things changed. Things started to get better. *I* started to get better. A magical solution didn't appear overnight that fixed everything, but it was like the weight that was crushing my chest and crusting my skin was finally being lifted. I was able to voice my hurts, fears, and hopes without thinking that I needed to have all the answers before my voice was valid. I finally felt like there was a sparkle of light at the end of what'd been a very damp, dark and long tunnel.

Day by day, after speaking with my husband and also seeing a homeopath, my skin started to clear up. The stress of keeping all that hurt and pain inside of my body had been reduced. Therefore, the inflammation, redness, and pain of my skin reduced, too. My skin became (and still is) a barometer for how much I'm holding inside that shouldn't be there. If something emotionally is "getting under my skin", then my actual skin tries to get my attention.

Your issue may not be your skin – it might be migraines, painful periods, tummy troubles, panic attacks – you must look at what's going on emotionally and not just deal with it physically. So, make sure if you're suffering with a physical symptom, as well as getting your physical health investigated, also ask yourself, "What's troubling me that I'm not speaking up about? Is there something I'm suppressing? Is there an emotion that needs to be moved through and out of my body?" In my experience as someone who specialises in women's health issues, there's more often than not always an emotional stressor involved in triggering or exacerbating physical problems.

**Ways To Speak Up**

I now realise I gave so much of my power away by not speaking up and instead was waiting for my husband to see and fix a situation I hadn't even told him about. It's sometimes easier to put the blame on others for our poor mental and/or physical health instead of realising we often hold the keys to help release ourselves from some of the prisons we find ourselves in. We can get angry believing that others should instinctively care for us more, know how we're feeling, notice we're tired, and struggling. However, this just adds fuel to the fire of our suppressed feelings and dis-ease. We have to start taking responsibility and speaking up for ourselves, taking care of ourselves, telling others how we're truly feeling and how we need them to help or support us. We have to break up with the victim or martyr mentality that I know I've been guilty of because it won't help you at all and only takes away your sparkle.

So, if you're waiting for someone else to see that you're tired, struggling, angry, needing help, a break, to cancel plans, more love, a raise, or are in pain in some way, don't remain quiet. It's *your* job to speak up for yourself to those around you, tell them your truth, and then do all you can to ensure you get what you need to stay in good mental and physical health. I can tell you from personal experience that not relying on someone else's telepathic abilities will dramatically boost your health, sparkle, and relationships.

**Here's a few ways that may help you …**

**Start Small**

I know if you're not used to it, the idea of speaking up for yourself and expressing your true feelings (after possibly decades of silencing them) is scary. So, I want you to start small. I want you to realise that speaking up for yourself isn't a new skill you need to learn – it's a skill and muscle you've always had but just not exercised enough. Maybe you don't know what you want to speak up about, or think that you don't have anything to speak up about. I promise you do!

Here's a small example. When you go to a restaurant with a friend and you're looking at the menu, if your friend asks what you're having do you speak up straight away or do you say, "Mmmm, I'm not sure… What are you having?" The thing is, you may think you don't know what you want from that menu, but I'm telling you, you do. When you look down at that menu, your body and mind make a choice almost immediately. It's instinctive.

It may be a cold day and you feel a bit under the weather, so your body wants something comforting and warm like soup with fresh bread. You may be craving something fatty, so you want the sweet potato chips with mayo. You may feel sluggish and your body wants a salad and fresh juice. You may be near your period and want extra carbs or a dessert. You may not even be genuinely hungry and just want something to drink. Your body knows exactly what it wants. However, many women aren't used to listening to their bodies and allowing them to speak up.

Women have been taught that their bodies and desires – especially when it comes to food – cannot be trusted. We can also worry what others might think. This leads to some 'in-spoken' conversations that may go something like this: "I said I was going to be "good" today, so I can't eat anything fatty," or "I don't want people thinking I'm greedy so I won't order that," or, "I don't know what my friend is having so I don't want to order a big meal in case they're just having something light."

All of this in-speaking makes you think you don't know what you want from the menu, but let me remind you that you know *exactly* what you want from that menu. You did the first time you looked at it, you just didn't know how to speak up for it. You're out of practice of expressing your needs and desires. So try it. Next time you're in a café or restaurant, don't put your menu choice through all the 'in-spoken' conversations and filters that try and make you insecure or worry about what other people think. Tune into your body, look at the menu, speak up, and order exactly what you blooming well want!

Also – I know you think if you do this that your body will order chips and dessert every time, but this simply isn't true – again this goes back to the lies women have been taught so that diet and fitness products can be sold to them. If you learn about different foods and the effect they have on your body, eat some of the really good sparkly stuff your body needs, understand and acknowledge that your appetite and desires will change throughout your cycle AND remember that your body is on your side and can be trusted (and you're not just not just a glutton whose appetite should be monitored and suppressed at all times) – your body will start to surprise you. Sometimes it'll pick the sweet treat or comforting carbs, but as many times it'll pick the salad, a juice and demand a big side of veggies.

## Write It Out

After years of not speaking up about the things really affecting you, you might find it easier to start expressing your emotions in writing – I know I did. This is still an important way of speaking up if you don't feel confident saying things face to face. It's also a great tool to help you move emotion through and out of your body – which is why journaling is so beneficial for women.

If someone has really upset or angered me, I often write them a letter saying exactly what I think about them and how hurt I am by them or the situation. Let me tell you, you'd be shocked if you read some of these letters because usually I swear and say really mean and petty things – I totally let rip with how I'm feeling. However, I don't ever send the letter. I just use it as a powerful (and free) tool to get all of that suppressed and pent up anger, frustration, and emotion out of my body instead of pretending that I'm "fine" or "over it" when really it's still all bubbling and festering inside of me. I find this such a good way to help you express all you've felt unable to let go of. It also frees up huge amounts of mental and physical energy in your body that's previously been spent going over and over the same situation and increasing your stress, annoyance and exhaustion.

I'd urge you to try this and *really* let loose when you use this type of letter writing. Be explicit about all of your feelings – I want you to shock yourself with the things that come out when you let out what you truly think and feel. Say everything you want to say. The phrase "be the bigger person" is often bandied about as an enlightened response to any hurt you've felt and not expressed or explored. I think to be the bigger person, you have to first be the smaller person.

Small people grow into bigger people. So, write your letter as the smallest, pettiest, angriest, meanest, most unkind person first (can you imagine as a woman being "allowed" to do this and not just encouraged to be sweet, nice, 'love and light' and ignore how you feel?!). I want you to express, not suppress, all of your emotions. *Then* you can be the bigger person and not send the letter.

To push down your feelings without ever moving all of that emotion out will exhaust and inflame your body and mind. It also belittles your experience of a situation and once more minimises your voice as a woman. Remember, the teachings of why you should be a "good" and "nice" woman who doesn't express her true feelings so others can feel comfortable will run deep, and so this can feel uncomfortable. However, this type of letter writing is the same as allowing steam to come out of a pressure cooker and once you've released this emotional "steam", then the normal pressure or balance within your own body and mind can be restored. If the steam, i.e. your rawest emotions, isn't released, it'll just build up to an explosion that has the potential to create physical or mental dis-ease. It's far better to release any powerful, hot, steam-filled emotions regularly and safely.

The next type of letter or email you can write is one that you *can* send to someone if you feel like you wouldn't be able to express yourself properly in person. I've done this many times when I've felt I didn't have the confidence or communication skills to properly explain my feelings or opinion about something important. In this instance, what I would say is write a first draft (it can be using the above "petty letter" so you get any anger, hurt, or annoyance out first if this is needed). Then wait at least 24-48 hours and write the letter again.

Ask yourself – what's my aim in sending this letter/ email? Will the way I've written it reach that aim? Keep this in mind and try to avoid pages and pages of aggression, ramblings, or outpouring of all your emotions (that's what the first draft is for). This is the time to yes speak up for yourself but, make it as short, precise, and to the point as possible. Do you want to just explain yourself? Do you want to give or ask for an apology? Is there another purpose for this letter? Do it succinctly and end it with the action of what you'd like the other person to take. For example, do you want them to write back to you, give you a call, or think it over? You may not get your desired outcome from the other person but, speaking up for what you've experienced and what you'd like to happen next, ensures you've done all you can to resolve the issue and get what you need to be able to move on in some way.

## Go Pro

Maybe your feelings are too deep, painful, or you don't feel comfortable speaking up to someone you know. If that's the case, then please find a recommended professional. There's nothing more wonderful than being completely open and honest with someone who can let you speak up without worrying if you're talking too much, what others might think, or if you've caused hurt or offence. We so rarely get to express our true feelings in this way, so it's no wonder it's called 'therapy'.

If you've experienced a mental or physical trauma that you've not spoken about and it affects your daily life, then when the time is right for you, you might want to look to speak with a recommended professional to help your mind and body heal. However, even if you've not experienced something that you'd describe as traumatic, a professional counsellor, therapist, or coach can still be a healing or helpful ally to work with.

Many of the clients I work with say they feel energised and 'lighter' after our sessions and this is before I've even given them any further information or diet/supplement/lifestyle advice on what I know can help them. And I've felt that too when I've been to various professionals to help me, I nearly always leave feeling lighter just from talking about things that were troubling me, even if I've not yet implemented any of their advice. This is because there can be immediate sparkle-boosting benefits for you when you move pushed down emotions out of your body and speak up for yourself.

### Things to Always Speak Up For...

### Your Health

I know you might think that the best person to understand your body is a medical professional with numerous degrees and a white coat, but it's not. It's actually you! In the same way you feel hunger or tiredness and know what those cues from your body mean, you've also been given unique knowledge about your body that expresses itself through your thoughts, gut feelings and instincts. So, if you feel like something is truly not right in your body but have been told there's nothing wrong, don't ever feel embarrassed for persisting in matters regarding your health (this applies to if you have children too – women and mother's intuition is real and powerful).

Maybe you've had some tests done and a doctor has said to you that all your tests have come back "normal", but you still feel unwell and like something's not right – trust yourself! Speak up for your health and decide to see a different doctor or an alternative health practitioner who will listen to your body's wisdom and not just tell you that you're fine when you don't feel fine. Do you remember what I said about bio-individuality earlier? Every single person is different, so this means that one person's "normal" from a medical test can be another person's "not living with optimal health and feel crappy".

The charts to decide what's a normal range for a certain health condition often haven't been updated for years. More often than not, these charts don't take into account your bio-individuality, hormonal fluctuations, or personal circumstances. Also, a blood test is like a photograph in that it only takes a "snapshot" of what was going on in your body at that moment. The next day, week, or after a stressful day or certain meal it can often show something different. So again, feel free to ask for more or different tests if you're still not feeling well after being told you're fine.

After years of working with women, I know that too many are brushed off (especially if it's to do with hormonal problems) when actually they need to be investigated and listened to further and not just told "it's normal" or sent away with another hormonal pill or anti-depressant to try (please remember I'm not against any woman choosing to use these, I'm just against these being prescribed instead of taking time to investigate the root cause of a woman's physical or mental struggle and listening to her speak up about her concerns).

We have to understand as women that we're paying for our healthcare (btw the NHS is not free – you pay for it through your taxes) so we're consumers, not beneficiaries of medical philanthropists. We're consumers who are paying for doctors and consultants and deserve to have the best service possible. Current healthcare systems are sadly failing too many women (especially from the BAME community) with men seen as the 'standard' for medical care. Meaning a lot of advice, drugs, and treatments are based on or geared for men and their bodies, with women often treated as a slight variant of that.

Women are different to men at a cellular level and sex differences have been found in every organ system and tissue in the body. Women generally suffer more from auto-immune diseases and anxiety than men, and have a different metabolic system to men. This means diabetes, drugs, alcohol, caffeine, diet and exercise all affect women differently. However, women have largely been excluded from medical research due to our 'hormonal variability', which can skew nice, neat drug trials, and research projects.

If women are used, they're often only tested in their follicular phase when they're hormonally most like men (although don't worry we account for over 90% of the participants used in trials for anti-wrinkle products, so that's wonderful to know isn't it?). Please, please, please go read Part IV 'Going to the doctor' in the book *Invisible Women; Exposing data bias in a world designed for men* by Caroline Criado Perez. I'm not exaggerating when I say the information in that part of the book could actually save your (or a female loved ones') life. The fact the medical system and many drugs, trials, and treatments are geared towards men will help you understand why you may still be suffering or being fobbed off after years in the medical system.

When I first went to the doctor about the lump in my breast, I was told it was likely just a cyst and nothing to worry about (just to say, with lots of breast lumps, this can actually be the case). However, my whole body felt uneasy and like something wasn't right. I then went to hospital to see a top breast consultant and have a biopsy. The biopsy came back clear and I was once again told that it was just a lump that posed no risk to my health.

However, my body and mind still felt uneasy and I felt strongly that I wanted this lump out of my body – this wasn't a feeling I'd previously ever experienced. I asked the consultant if I could have the lump removed anyway because it didn't feel right, and he made me feel really foolish and embarrassed for even discussing it because "there was no need". But, I listened to my body, spoke up for it, and booked to see a different consultant who listened to me and said that if I wanted to, I could of course have surgery to remove the lump.

He then gave me two options of how to remove the lump. One was to have it broken up in my body and sucked out through a tiny aspirator (this would only leave a pinprick of a scar on my chest so was the most preferable thing to do in this instance with a supposed 'normal' lump). The second option I was given was that I could be cut across my breast and have the lump cut out "cleanly", but this would leave a more significant scar. The logical choice would of course been the first option, but my body didn't feel at peace when I thought about it. I asked the consultant what I should do. He said, "Sleep on it and when you wake up in the morning, you'll know what to do." What an amazing consultant! He'd given me back my power and shown me that a decision about *my* body could be made by *my* body's wisdom. I woke up the next day and opted for the surgery to have the lump cut out in its entirety.

As soon as I was booked in for the surgery, I felt a huge sense of relief. You can imagine how many people thought it was strange to be having an operation to remove something doctors had said was fine, as well as choosing the option that would leave the greatest scar on my body. But, I somehow knew, probably for the first time in my life, that my body should be listened to. The operation was a success and I felt a huge sense of relief that the lump was out of my body. Two weeks later, when I went in to see my consultant so he could check my scar, he sat me down with a shocked face and said, "Well, all I can say is that someone "up there" must be looking out for you."

He went on to explain the lab report had shown that I had a rare tumour and would need to be booked in immediately for a second operation to remove more breast tissue to make sure it hadn't spread. He explained that had I have chosen the first, less superficially invasive procedure for the lump removal it would've spread the tumour cells throughout my breast and we'd be looking at "an entirely different and very serious prognosis". Because I'd chosen the seemingly more invasive but "clean" removal of the tumour, I'd now likely just need a second operation to remove more breast tissue as opposed to a partial or full mastectomy. I cried and cried until I was out of breath. Yes, I was sad that I needed further surgery, but I cried mostly because of the wisdom of my body. It wasn't someone "up there" looking out for me (because I don't believe God is "up there"), it was something "in me" (which, in my belief is where God, or whatever you call your connection to the Divine, resides).

I believe, inside every woman, guiding you through your intuition and gut feelings, that you've been trained to ignore or belittle, is a powerful source that has more wisdom about you than the highest medical professional in the world. If you genuinely feel that something's wrong, don't ever accept being told it's not. You know your body. Why is it we would trust that the owner of a dog, house, or car would be the best person to tell us what's going on with any of those things BUT not the owner of a body?

I'm not against doctors. There are some truly amazing ones who love, nurture, and save lives. Sadly, there are also ones who ignore, dismiss, and patronise many women and what they're seeking help for. Don't ever discount or belittle your own wisdom, gut instincts, or feelings about your body, no matter how small the whisper is. Your wisdom and feelings *can* be trusted. Speak up for your health as many times as you need to – even if your voice shakes. Don't let anyone brush you off and tell you that you're not in pain or are just imagining it or should put up with something that's draining you or a drug that's making you feel horrible. Speak up until you feel well, and don't you dare settle for feeling crappy and sparkle-less when you deserve health and happiness.

## Your Inner Wisdom

If you don't believe in spiritual things or have your own spiritual practice, then you may think this sounds a bit 'woo-woo'. However, I'm telling you there's a sparkly spiritual side to us all. It's an inner wisdom you were born with and will help guide you until the day you die. It just needs you to take a moment to listen to it and not dismiss it.

Your inner wisdom carries the divine blueprint of who you truly are and were created to be. It enables you to connect to something outside of your own logic where you can find divine help for earthly struggles. It doesn't matter what your individual religion or spiritual practice is or isn't, because I know for sure you'll have already experienced your inner wisdom. Perhaps without even knowing it.

Did you know that your intuition and gut feelings that you have but often ignore or dismiss as "a silly thought" *is* your inner wisdom in dialogue with you? It's your spirit within, reminding you that you weren't created to be exhausted, disillusioned, and depressed. It makes you long for a better way of living. It encourages you to pick up books like this one and find your way back to your true self and sparkle. It nudges you to hope and believe that there's help out there for you no matter how long you've been struggling for so you could live with the energy, confidence, passion, and purpose deep down you know you're meant to. Your inner wisdom can make you feel uneasy about and question certain things that others tell you to be certain of. Have you ever experienced that? It's a knowledge that seems to come from outside of you, but is within you.

Don't get caught up with names, either. Some people will call their inner wisdom God (which is my preferred name and the one that resonates in my sparkly spirit the most), others the Divine, Creator, or a religion-specific name. It's more important that you acknowledge that you have this sparkly inner wisdom that you can connect with, listen to, call upon, and speak up for, than reject it because of a name you disagree with or has negative connotations for you.

You have to understand that the same powerful force that created this whole universe resides in your cells and interacts with you every moment of every day. You – not a guru, priest, or other self-declared spiritual guide – are most able to tune into your inner wisdom. Just taking five minutes for yourself or by prayer, journaling, meditation, reflection, or whatever works for you can help you connect with your inner wisdom. This inner wisdom can help you work out what you need to live your most authentic and happy life. Divine guidance isn't reserved for religious or wacky people, it's there for you every day. Check in with your "gut feelings" daily about various situations, even though you've been taught to champion the male-centred 'logic and reason'. It's there to always help you get your sparkle back.

Here's some promptings your inner wisdom may have already given you that you didn't realise were your own divine whispers nudging you back to your health, happiness, and sparkle:

- Your inner wisdom whispers, "You're exhausted. You need to start taking more time to rest before you burn out or get sick." But you argue back, "What's wrong with me? I'm always tired. There's no time to rest because no one else will do all the things that need to get done today. I just need a strong coffee and to crack on."

- Your inner wisdom knows your body and whispers, "You're hungry and in need of some proper nourishment today." Your response is, "What's wrong with me?! I'm always hungry and meant to be on a diet because I'm so fat and disgusting! I just need to have more willpower and ignore my body."

- Your inner wisdom whispers, "You hate this job, it makes you feel so down and uses none of your talents and gifts. If you only live once why not start pursuing the things you long to do?" You immediately bat away this prompt with the supposed logic of, "There's no way *I* can have a career change. I'm too old and don't have the money or qualifications. This is the real world, not a dream life."

Every time you ignore the prompts or disbelieve your inner wisdom, you disconnect further from your true self and sparkle. If you don't believe that your inner wisdom is a truth-filled guide and instead believe that your hopes, dreams, and best life are just a childish fantasy, then, like a child who's always told to "shut up" or "get real", the nudges of your inner wisdom will get quieter. Eventually, you'll start saying things like, "I don't know who I am, what I want from life, or how to be happy," because you've lost touch with the divine light that was always trying to guide you back to your sparkle

Thankfully, you can heal, nurture, listen to and speak up for your sparkly inner wisdom. When you hear the whisper of, "I'm really exhausted and I don't think I can go out tonight," you can speak up, cancel plans, and tell everyone you're going to bed early instead since that's what your body needs. When you feel your inner wisdom reminding you, "I'm so unhappy in this job," you can speak up, ask someone for some mentoring or advice, start researching the things you want to do, and believe there are better ways to earn money and pursue your dreams.

When you sense your inner wisdom alerting your body to the fact that, "I'm hungry," or "I'm thirsty," you can thank your body for that information and believe its wisdom to act upon, rather than steamroller over it because you're too busy and others need you. Listen to and speak up for your inner wisdom because it's your own divine GPS that's always guiding you back to the path back of your best self, health and brightest sparkle.

## Daily Sparkle Habits

There'll be some simple things, unique to you, that'd help you to truly sparkle every day. For some women, it'll be having a cup of tea in peace, going for a walk alone, doing yoga, or not cooking dinner every night. For others, it'll be going to the gym, having a bath, drinking a homemade smoothie, watching a TV show that no one else likes, or going out with a friend. Only *you* know the things that you need in your daily life to make you happy and sparkle. So, it's time to speak up for those things and treat them as non-negotiables instead of luxuries because they're your personal sparkle-boosting strategies.

For me, every day I need to get outside in the fresh air, have at least 30 minutes alone with no one bothering me, and eat at least one or two meals that are nutritious and bursting with health and vitality. If these things are removed from my day too often, I end up feeling super crappy and not sparkly at all. It affects me and therefore all those around me. But, I have to speak up for myself and tell the people around me that I need these things daily so they won't be surprised or unknowingly sabotage them to get what they need from me instead.

I have to loudly speak up for my daily sparkle habits. Otherwise they won't happen. I have to decline calls, not respond immediately to demands/requests/invites and say "no" every day so I get these things. These daily sparkle habits are like medicine for myself and sparkle. So, what are some of the daily sparkle habits that *you* need to speak up for to improve your health and happiness? What daily habits would boost your sparkle tenfold if they were included in your everyday life? What daily habits are you hoping and planning to do when you have more time/money/someone else to see you need them, when some you could start today?

Do you need to take a walk around the block on your own to clear your head from household or office chaos, go for a run, do some yoga, lie down for 10 minutes, have a warm not cold cup of tea? Then speak up for yourself and make this as normal part of your day as brushing your teeth. Does having a bath boost your body, mind, and spirit? Then speak up to your family and let them know that there'll be no access to you or the bathroom between certain times on certain days – and make it non-negotiable. Remember this is your sparkle medicine! If you wouldn't let those around you throw pills away you'd been prescribed for your health and happiness, don't let them throw away these daily sparkle habits you need. Would you love time for a new hobby, to see a friend, or start a course? Then decide it's time to speak up and tell people that you're going to do it!

Stop feeling bad about speaking up for the things that give you even the smallest amount of energy, joy, peace and daily sparkle. You'll not only benefit from this, but all those around you will get to enjoy your extra glow and sparkle too instead of your anger, frustration, or exhaustion. Remember, people aren't mind readers. If you don't tell them what you need in your day to feel balanced and happy, then they'll be too busy with their own lives or benefit too much from how you usually behave to care that your cup of tea went cold or you missed your dance class for the third week running. Speak up for your daily sparkle habits, life will start to feel so much better, once you do.

## Your Sparkly Story

One of the biggest reasons for you to start speaking up is because whether you realise it or not, you have a message that others need to hear. We all do. The formula for your message is normally this: the tough and crappy stuff you've been through (i.e. the mess) + your age = your message. I'm telling you, your message will be able to help and inspire others. It may help or heal one person on one particular day in your life, or it may be there for the whole world to access all the time. Either way, you have to know that there's power and a purpose for what you've been through. You may speak up and share your sparkle-boosting story with a friend over coffee and give her hope when she's feeling hopeless or you may write a book that speaks to lots of people – both are as valuable and important as the other.

I have a 3 ½ inch scar on my chest from my breast tumour operations and, for a long time, that scar made me cry every time I saw it. It was a constant reminder that the happy, free-spirited, sparkly version of me was gone for good. I felt I'd been replaced by a fragile, unhappy, scared (and scarred) version of me – and I hated it. It reminded me of being ill and I didn't want a reminder of that. But let me tell you, I love my scar now. I'm serious. Yes, it took time, years actually (so don't feel bad if you're not there yet), but that scar no longer says sadness to me. It used to say, "Well done, you survived". Now it says, "Hey sparkle pants, it's time to bloody thrive!" It represents a second chance at a life I'd taken for granted and lost my true self and sparkle in.

I've been through the pain that many of you have been through – the death of loved ones, disease, debt, depression, men breaking up with me, friends breaking up with me, business associates cheating me. But all this mess holds my message. My sparkle and scars live side-by-side. One does not cancel out the other.

I love the Japanese practice of 'Kintsugi' where if an item of pottery is broken, it's not repaired using invisible glue to camouflage what's happened (which is what we're kind of taught to do as women, hide our pain and brokenness). Gold, silver, or platinum are used in the repair process to highlight the cracks, add sparkle to them, and show how there's now a new value and beauty to the piece that wasn't there before. I definitely know that there's gold and sparkle woven into the scars on my body and mind. That my value has only increased, not been shattered. I don't want or need invisible glue holding me together, because I don't ever have to pretend that nothing bad has ever happened to me. I can have visible scars and still be whole and sparkle again.

At the right time and only it feels right for you, then speak up and share your message no matter how big or small.

Your story of sadness or loss can become a message of hope, encouragement, and healing for someone else. Your story of finding freedom will help someone who feels trapped. Your story of getting better – mentally or physically – can inspire someone who's suffering and ill. Don't ever think your pain was pointless although, in the midst of it, I know that's exactly how it feels and don't let anyone try and tell you while you're in the middle of your suffering or struggle that it's all for a "good reason" and needs to be used to help others. That is so hurtful and harmful.

Don't ever think that you have nothing to give to this world, because you do. I love the analogy of tapestries – have you ever seen the back of one? It's a big old mess – clumsy knots and cut pieces of thread. But, on the other side, it's the most beautiful picture. Sometimes we spend so long looking at the "knotted mess" of our life we can forget to look at the other side where a truly magnificent story and piece of art has been created. So, at the right time, and only if you want to, speak up. You and your story, your mess and your message (no matter how big or small) are needed to help one person or a million women get their sparkle back.

## You'll Be A Dazzling Disappointment

A quick heads up. When you start to speak up for yourself and not suppress your emotions, I believe, your mental and physical health and overall sparkle will improve. However, I want to warn you that you might become a dazzling disappointment to other people.

There are some things in life that'll *always* happen. Jumping up in the air will always result in you coming back down again. Putting your hand in a fire will result in a burn. Speaking up to get your sparkle back will always disappoint some people. To live as the healthiest, happiest, most confident, energised, sparkly version of yourself, you *must* disappoint some people in your life.

I know you might think that making a few changes to boost yourself and speaking up for your needs won't disappoint people, but it will. It always does. Of course, they'll be some people who're super pleased you're pursing your own health and happiness after years of ignoring it. However, there'll be people who want to meet up with you when you're on your period (a time when you need lots of rest) and they'll be disappointed when you choose to speak up for your health, not burnout, instead of seeing them. You'll disappoint the boss who tries to give you more work, but you speak up and say, "no," because you're at full capacity or want to leave work on time to see your family. You'll disappoint a client who's previously enjoyed having you on call 24/7, but you've now spoken up and created better boundaries. You'll disappoint your partner or other members of your family when you speak up to say there are some things you want to change so your needs are no longer put last. The list of potential disappointments is endless. But, guess what? You'll be okay!

Can you see how none of the above scenarios are wrong and that you're not being a bad person, even though you might be made to feel like one? Can you see that your mental and physical health relies on you speaking up and disappointing some people, some of the time – even those you deeply love and want to make happy? Can you see that you've been conditioned not to speak up for your health, needs, dreams? Speaking up and disappointing people is actually part and parcel of getting your sparkle back and reaching your full potential in life.

I know it feels better initially not to disappoint people, but it's literally impossible to live a happy, successful, authentic, or sparkle-filled life if you don't make peace with the fact that disappointing people *will* happen. I'm not talking about consistent, malicious behaviour. I'm talking about speaking up for your energy, health, and the things that matter deeply to you. The root of not wanting to disappoint people lies in wanting to be liked and well thought of. I get it. I was the biggest people pleaser out there before I got ill. But, long-term people-pleasing is stressful and dangerous because all people can't be pleased all the time. You'll exhaust yourself or make yourself ill trying.

Each time you think, hear, or feel someone's disappointment, you'll feel uncomfortable for sure. It's like training a muscle – it'll burn, feel too much and you'll want to give up. But, keep going. Take that as a sign you've chosen your sparkle and purpose over constant people-pleasing. Keep speaking up about all you need to. Step back into the power of being a woman who speaks up for herself so she can sparkle brightly while she's on this earth.

Your own health and life rely on you growing in confidence and speaking up for yourself. And so do the lives of others. If you learn how to stand up and speak up for yourself then you can start to speak up for others who can't speak up or are simply not heard due to their circumstances or the inequalities that exist in this world. Your voice can ensure not only the health, safety, rights, and happiness of you and your loves ones, but those of other women or people in need in your community and around the world. Women are one of the most powerful resources in this world – there are so many things that we can change for good – but, we must first begin to speak up. We've been silent for too long and the world is a worse and more unequal place because of it. Speak up for yourself, so you can then speak up for (and help amplify the voices of) those who need to be heard most at this time – which in my opinion is particularly the voices and experiences of non-white women.

### 2 Small Sparkly Steps For Today...

1) This evening I want you to speak up for what you want for dinner. Do you want beans on toast because you can't be bothered to cook or a roast dinner with all the trimmings, and you want other people to cook it for you? Do you want a salad, a takeaway, a friend to go out to dinner with you? Enjoy the feeling that comes from getting something you desire that you wouldn't normally speak up for because you didn't want to bother others or thought their opinions/wants/needs should always be put before yours.

2) What's one personal or global situation that you'd like to have the confidence to speak up on? Think about 3 things you can do that'll help you do this – do you need to write a letter? Look for a counsellor? Do some research and read a book on the subject? Make some small steps on your journey of speaking up for your sparkle and others' too.

*NB: This chapter is aimed at helping women speak up for themselves on a daily basis and stop them suffering from the mental and physical consequences of not expressing who they are and how they truly feel. If you've experienced mental, physical, or sexual abuse and have not spoken-up about it to anyone, then please seek out a professional who can guide you carefully through this process and keep you safe.*

*Your GP should be able to advise you about this process, or you can look up local charities or counselling organisations. Most importantly, be gentle with yourself. Make sure you feel comfortable and safe with the professional you have chosen, and go at your own pace to free yourself from the silence and any shame that's been put on you. Don't let anyone force you to speak up about what you've gone through. That's entirely up to you and should never be done unless you want or are ready to. Please remember, regardless of what has been done to you or how anyone has made you feel, you're a beautiful, treasured, perfect, precious woman with sparkle and have a unique purpose for being on this earth. Sending you the biggest sparkle-filled hug wherever you are today.*

# SECRET OF
# YOUR SPARKLE

Wow, what a journey we've been on together to get your sparkle back. So, it's now time to learn about what I believe is the absolute secret of your sparkle and, funnily enough, that starts with a lot of unlearning! You see, this book isn't just about getting your sparkle back; it's about you being able to keep it for the rest of your life. I want to encourage you to stop living as the smallest, unworthiest, self-hating, self-deprecating, ashamed, ignored, guilt-ridden, unfulfilled, 2-D, black and white, apologising, people-pleasing, fearful, watered-down, hopeless, pleasure-less, dreamless, exhausted version of yourself. And instead, enter a new chapter where from now on your decide to take the smallest of steps or biggest of leaps and start living as the healthiest, truest, brightest, boldest, most unashamed, authentic, energised, excited, outrageous, fulfilled, fun-filled, sexy, sassy, spirited, 3-D, multi-coloured, purpose-pursuing, hope-filled, pleasure-filled, vision-filled, sparkle-filled version of yourself. Basically – the real you – the one you were always created to be.

Getting your sparkle back is simply about returning to your true self. And I believe the secret of you being able to do that comes from loving and being who you truly are. I know when you're urged to "just be yourself" or "love yourself" it can feel like the most unachievable ideal – I know it did for me. Maybe you don't know how to be yourself, don't want to be yourself, or don't have the energy to try. It's hard when you may have spent a lifetime not feeling good enough and possibly wishing you were someone else. I promise being your true self will be the thing to help make your dreams come true. The thing that makes your sparkle shine brightest.

If you feel like loving and being your true self is an impossible feat, I get it. I used to hate myself. I genuinely hated how I looked. I didn't know who the real me was and I lived as multiple versions of myself to try and please or appease those around me. For decades, with each new job, relationship, or situation, I'd morph into a different version of myself, hoping that *this* version would be liked, loved, or I'd find the approval I was desperate for. I wore myself out and made myself ill trying to be so many different things to different people. However, I eventually found my way back to myself, which brought my sparkle back and, I'm telling you, you can do the same.

This chapter is essentially a 'factory reset' for you. You weren't born to try and live as, want to be, or look like someone else. You weren't created to constantly dislike, change or hide parts of yourself or feel like a permanent disappointment to yourself or others. You weren't meant to drag yourself through each day only to feel just as crappy the next. Your purpose isn't to constantly meet the needs of others and neglect your own. You weren't given your unique body to be ashamed of it, ignore it, or drive yourself to exhaustion in the endless pursuit of trying to change, "better" or "perfect" it. You weren't given your dreams and passions just to be taunted by them your whole life. You were given them as signposts to your happiness, sparkle, and things you're meant to do on this earth.

A woman who's comfortable and confident with herself and her body is a sparkly force to be reckoned with. I'm telling you, a big part of your tiredness and lack of vitality isn't just to do with how you sleep and what you eat. Your sparkle is suffering because you're using up huge amounts of energy being at war with yourself instead of happily living with and loving who you are. It's time to come home to you.

Before I nudge you forward to a place you may have never thought possible – where you swap feeling shameful about yourself for feeling special and where your body is a delight and not a disappointment – we need to go back and ask how did you get here? How did you and I and so many other women end up feeling so crappy (to put it mildly) about ourselves and lose our sparkle in the process?

## What You've Been Taught Is Wrong

The origins of why you may not like, let alone love yourself, might feel big and complicated. Yet, it's far simpler than you think. The reason you feel so crappy about yourself is… you've been taught to! From a young age, from all different places and people, you've been taught, openly and subliminally, that who you are, how you look, and even often what you think is wrong. You've been taught that your body shouldn't visibly get older past the age of about 25, change, grow in size or have any texture or blemishes. It's not meant to display proudly that it's grown children, survived operations or accidents and it certainly can't be sexy over a certain age. Coupled with being bombarded with messages about how flawed your body is, you've been taught that people-pleasing and being in constant service to others is a wonderful trait for a woman to have. That caring for others and adapting to their needs and ignoring your own – even if you end up stressed, burnt out and ill – is seen as a truly beautiful way for a woman to live and die.

I'm guessing, like me, your sparkle was given away piece by piece, and it was done so slowly you didn't even realise till you looked in the mirror and didn't recognise the sparkle-less woman staring back at you. Your innate power to reach your highest potential, purpose, and goals has been silently traded, without your knowledge or permission, for self-hatred, insecurity, exhaustion, and anxiety.

Well, no more my sparkle sister! It's time to go to 'Sparkle School' and do some serious unlearning. It's time to take back your knowledge, power, body, and sparkle for good!

# Sparkle School – Where We Unlearn The Lies

We're going to go through six sparkly lessons to help you unlearn some of the biggest lies that you've been taught about your body and self. I totally believe in the power of good food and hydration to revolutionise and boost women's bodies and lives. However, over the years, I've personally seen that no amount of greens or superfoods can replace the energising, healing, and sparkle-boosting effects that loving, liking, or at least being kinder to yourself can bring.

The reason I believe we're meant to love ourselves and our bodies (and not just tolerate, accept, or ignore them) is that we're in a life-long relationship with them. If you don't think a child or partner deserves you to hate, ignore, or be neutral towards them, then why should your body? If you think about how stressful it is or would be to live in the same house as someone you hate, who says vile and horrible things to you all the time, think how stressed (and therefore inflamed) your body is from your constant self-loathing and trash talk to it?

Feelings of 'body neutrality' or acceptance may be vital steps in you reaching the goal of loving yourself if you're starting from a place of self-hatred. I personally don't think it should end there. Love helps us grow. Love helps us heal. Loving ourselves helps others love their selves. Love puts a light in our eyes and spring in our step. That's why I believe you should get to experience loving yourself (even if it's not every day) because it can get your sparkle back and keep it there!

I'd suggest reading each of the below lessons one at a time and then taking a short break to ponder on what you've started to unlearn. Then, take a moment to do your Sparkle School homework and see how your body and mind reacts to information that's the opposite of what it's been bombarded with for decades. Ding, ding. Class is starting…

## Lesson 1

### UNLEARN: You're nothing special.

I'm not going to tell you that I think you're absolutely amazing and you should think this too because it may sound disingenuous or like a generic inspirational quote you don't believe or connect with. Instead, let's just start with some basic facts that can't be argued with – like the fact you're an actual miracle. Yep. That's not a fluffy, motivational pep talk – that's a fact.

You're a true odds-defying, once-in-a-lifetime miracle. Statistically, you and that body of yours shouldn't exist. The actual chance of being alive and experiencing life as a human is about 1 in 400 trillion. Do you know how huge that is? A trillion is about 1,000 billion (and there's 1000 million in a billion! I know, I can't get my head around numbers that big, either). You actually began your life as a winner – someone who beat the 1 in 400 trillion odds of the exact egg from one person selecting a specific sperm from another, successfully growing from a fetus into a baby and then actually being born. It's a truly unbelievable and statistically mind-blowing, chain of events resulting in you being here. There's literally more chance of you winning the lottery – which is a mere 1 in 14 million(ish).

So, whether you feel it today or not, you need to start getting your head around the fact that you're a walking, talking, sparkle-filled miracle who's meant to be here and has a purpose. Can you imagine how precious you'd think something was if you owned it and there was only a 1 in 400 trillion chance of it ever being made or existing? That's you! That's your body. That's your life. There's no auction price that exists that could actually match your worth. You've defied the odds that were stacked against you of walking on this earth and taking up space. There's nothing and no one like you in the whole universe, nor will there ever be again. But, I'm guessing, you still believe that you're nothing special, or your body's gross, or that your life's pretty "blah", boring, and not going anywhere?

My darling sparkle sister – hear me when I say… you're not a mess – you're a genuine miracle!

Let's just imagine for a moment that you started to own the truth of this fact instead of agreeing with the media or other messages that've made you believe you don't measure up. Just think how you could silence those voices in your head (we all have them) that constantly tell you compared to other women you're fat, ugly, boring, not good enough, not doing enough, or whatever the words are that you get tormented by. Imagine how you'd dress and walk and carry yourself each day if you grasped your true worth and unique value. Imagine the jobs you'd apply for or goals you'd go for. Imagine the relationships you'd no longer allow in your life. Imagine how good it'd feel to be you and be alive.

Well, I'm hoping that even just for one moment you'll stop imagining and start trying it on for size. When you look in the mirror and the crappy voice in your head wants to tell you you're worthless or don't measure up, start reminding yourself that you're a 1 in 400 trillion miracle of a person. Acknowledge as fact that your existence is special and an actual miracle. Attempt to believe that and feel like that for one minute a day, then 10 minutes the next day, then an hour the next week, then decide to try and spend a whole day bathing in this knowledge. I want you to unlearn all the BS that's kept you small and I want you to walk around like you're something special (and of course sparkly) – because guess what? Spiritually, emotionally, physically, and factually – you are! You, my darling, are not a mess, you're a miracle.

**Sparkle school homework** – Take one minute to shut your eyes and think of one process or function of your body that you think is miraculous? Now, put your hand on your heart, take a deep breath in through your nose and out through your mouth and say (in your head or out loud) "Wow, I'm a miracle".

## Lesson 2

### UNLEARN: Your body is a collection of flawed parts.

Without even realising it, you've most likely been treating your body like it's just a collection of different problem parts. It's not your fault. Some men, companies, as well as the medical profession and media have carved you up into various parts (just like those pictures of cows that show the different cuts of meat) for their consumption and profit. You've been told what's "okay" on you and what needs to be fixed. It was never meant to be like this.

You are a divine being far more precious than to exist as a sum of parts, full of shame and scrutiny. You're not a piece of meat that needs to be made palatable and delectable for a man's (or anyone's) consumption. You don't have good parts and bad parts. You're not to have your insecurities used and abused for others profit. You don't have separate, unconnected body parts that don't speak to each other and should be "treated" or medicated in isolation. You are a Queen, plain and simple. The human race wouldn't exist without you and your fellow Queens. It's about time you were treated, and treated yourself, as such. Stop thinking you need to constantly change or hide yourself. You were born to be seen and shine. So, let's go through some of the parts that women have been made to hate, encouraged to change and see what needs to be unlearnt.

**Your Beautiful Face**

It breaks my heart to say it now, but I didn't used to like my face. I always felt like my face was the reason I didn't get the jobs I wanted or the boys I fancied. I didn't have the high cheekbones of the '90s supermodels or the elfin features of the girls that all the boys seemed to drool over at school. I had round chubby cheeks, wonky teeth, and a scar in the middle of my forehead. I believed for many, many years that my face had been created a bit wrong.

An ex-boyfriend once asked me if I could change any part of my body what it would be (I now know I'd just change the boyfriend who asked me that question). I remember his horror when, without missing a beat, I said "my face". "Why?" he asked. "Because if I had a prettier face, my life would be easier" – that's what I genuinely thought! I'd been subliminally taught that if my face didn't look like the faces in magazines, on TV, or like the popular girls I knew, then it was obviously wrong. I want to go back now, hug that girl, show her a mirror (not the skewed one she had in her mind) and say, "You're the most perfect version of you that there'll ever be!"

For years, I battled with what I saw in the mirror. This wasn't helped by the fact that throughout my early 20s I was auditioning for backing dancing and TV presenting jobs. Every time I didn't get one, I was sure it was because my face was too ugly and my body too fat. Then one day, literally out of the blue, I had an epiphany about my face. I suddenly realised that it was meant to look exactly the way it did. I realised that my purpose and the people who are meant to be in my life will recognise me by who I truly am, and that includes what my face looks like. In the same way that different flowers are different colours and shapes to attract different insects – I'm meant to look like this so that everything and every person that's meant for me, can find me.

I no longer hate my face, believe my life would be better if it looked different, or want to look like someone else. I no longer think I can only be seen with a bucket load of make-up on (although I still love the creativity and art of make-up). I no longer scrutinise my lines and scars and think they're wrong. Sure, I have bad days where the negative voices tell me my face is wrong, but I don't listen to them for hours on end like I used to. I just tell them their opinion is so 1999 and a little outdated. I realise that a sunflower isn't unattractive because it doesn't look like a rose, and I'm not unattractive because I don't look like a celebrity or a woman from a magazine or polished Instagram account – that's just what I was trained to believe by the skewed and male-created beauty ideals of this world.

I actually unlearned the habit I had of looking in the mirror every day and immediately saying, "yuck," or "urgh," or "you look tired/gross/old." I finally saw how damaging this was and thought if I wouldn't stand behind my best friend or a child and say those things when they looked in the mirror, then I shouldn't say those things to myself. So, now I wake up every day and, even after all those years of criticising my face on a daily basis, I can now look in the mirror and say, "Look how cute you look!" I've decided that if a baby or animal can look tired, have a scrunched-up face and still be cute, then so can I.

It took a while, and I didn't believe it over night because my brain had to unlearn my pattern of saying hateful things to myself every day. In time though, I did unlearn it. I now genuinely believe that my face is unique, fabulous, and is allowed to have lines, texture, and pores.

I hope you start to unlearn the horrible things you've thought, said, or still say about your face. I hope you know that with or without make-up, you're perfect. That with or without a filter for your pictures, you're still flawless because by the way, women's supposed "flaws" were created by companies so they could make money from you. I recommend you read 'The Beauty Myth' by Naomi Wolf if you want to find out the history and coordinated campaign behind making women feel so crappy about themselves so companies could profit from it.

Like I said before, your face is allowed to age. You're allowed to look tired. Those lines around your eyes aren't wrinkles or 'crows feet' (these are just negative words again created to encourage you to buy expensive creams or procedures – I mean 'crows feet'! Not even flamingo or peacock feet, crows!). Those lines around your eyes are 'sparkle lines' and, just like the sun emits sunbeams to spread its light, your 'sparkle lines' shine out of your eyes to spread your light. So, the next time you see those lines around your eyes, don't despair and think something horrible about yourself. Smile even wider, run your finger along them and say "Oooh, look at my super cute sparkle lines." Behaviour like this is radical and revolutionary and a 'fingers up' to the people who've had actual meetings to work out how they can tell you about the "problems" of your body, so they can then sell you the "solution".

It's time to unlearn the horrible things you've said to yourself. Look at your face and say nice things to it every day. You won't believe them at first because you've been trained to see faults and flaws. But, start saying nice things about your face for 40 days and I promise you, you'll soon start to believe them. The bonus is that your eyes will sparkle more and you'll look even more gorgeous just by liking and not loathing your fabulous face. Can I also recommend reading the book *Mirror Work: 21 days to heal your life* by Louise Hay because it truly did help me start to like and love what I saw in the mirror after decades of not.

## Arms

Years ago, before I got married, I had a list of all the things I needed to change and work on to look like the allegedly 'perfect' bride. My arms were high up on that list as they'd always been soft and rounded, not muscly and sculpted like I'd been trained to believe they should be. However, when I got engaged and planned to marry 18 months later, circumstances quickly changed and we brought our wedding forward by twelve months. I remember panicking that I didn't have time to get arms like the brides in all the wedding magazines. I didn't have time to train like an athlete and change the natural shape of my arms. So, shock-horror, they stayed the way they were – soft and rounded, rather than slender and rock hard. When I look at my wedding pictures now, I realise there wasn't one thing wrong with my arms. But, because women have been told their arms are meant to look a certain way to be acceptable or attractive, I worried constantly about the un-athletic appearance of my arms in the run up to my wedding day.

We've got to stop and ask who has taught us so relentlessly that only toned arms with no texture on the skin are beautiful and correct? Like everything in life, variety exists. Some arms are long and lean, some are super toned, some are rounder with more flesh, but none of them are wrong. Also, arms have two parts – an upper and lower part. The upper part is naturally bigger than the lower part (basically an arm thigh if you will), but we always look at this part as if it should be as slim as the lower part. Most arms move and jiggle when you wave or dance. It doesn't mean you have to call them "bingo wings" or "dinner lady arms" because these "jokes" we have about various parts of women's bodies are actually more damaging than they are funny. We've got to stop feeling ashamed of our flesh – it's allowed and meant to move.

From picking up your child, cuddling a loved one, to cartwheeling (yes, let's get back to cartwheeling and feeling carefree), your arms are pretty incredible. Don't be told you can only wear certain things or show your arms off if they look like an athlete's or a celebrity's. Your body and arms are allowed to be soft if that's their natural look. You've been taught for decades that soft arms or thighs or tummies are wrong, unsexy, and mean you need to go to the gym.

If your lifestyle, hobbies and marvellous movement mean that your arms are toned – then that's fabulous. Just know that they don't *have* to be toned to be healthy or attractive. Can you imagine how free you'd feel if your exercise habits were just about you having fun and feeling vibrant, healthy, and full of sparkle instead of the tyranny of "toning-up"? Imagine if you sought out movement that lights you up instead of lightens you up. Imagine if you were told by the media and it shouted from the rooftops from a young age that "softness is sexy" as well as "toned is terrific". I think you're meant to enjoy that freedom.

I've been a professional dancer, a 'gym-a-holic' and also taken time off any form of exercise where my arms are used. My arms don't really change. They pretty much stay soft and rounded so, I've decided I'm not going to waste my life trying to change them. What about you? Why not lift your gorgeous arm in the air and give me a hi-5 to letting your arms look and move anyway they want to.

## Breasts

Time to tackle the unlearning that needs to be done about your breasts. Let's start by talking about the "fact" that round and perky breasts with no blemishes or marks are supposed to be the most attractive. For too long, this "ideal" breast shape has been dictated by the billion-dollar porn industry, where the look of identical, quasi-teenage breasts reigns supreme. How about we reclaim our breasts and not let the adult entertainment or plastic surgery industries lie to us and make us believe there's one type of boob that's better than another. Let's not believe our breasts exist just to tit-illate the opposite sex.

How's this for some new, not well-publicised information – your breasts are allowed to change over your lifetime. Yes, breasts and nipples are allowed to grow and shrink and get more texture and change colour. There's not one perfect size, shape, or colour of breasts. They can be round, pointy, big, small, long, flat. Some have stretch marks or scars. Some have nipples the size of smarties, others the size of saucers, others are inverted. Some nipples are pink, some purple, some brown, some black, some tattooed and once again, this variety should be displayed and enjoyed, not airbrushed and eradicated by the media.

Quite simply, all breasts should be seen, celebrated, and championed. Let's stop the jokes about boobs being saggy or droopy or needing a boob job because you're once again playing into the hands of (largely male-owned) companies looking to make you insecure, take your money, and change your appearance so you're more attractive to the male-gaze. Furthermore, let's stop aspiring to have the boobs of a teenager simply because that's what popular culture has trained men to desire and women to provide.

Why should women who've fed children, fought cancer, or lived a fabulous life be made to feel like their boobs (or lack of) are wrong? Why are we being sold bras that shape our boobs into the allegedly "right" shape and size (ever wondered why so many bras are padded and round and push up your boobs – it's not for your benefit)? Can you imagine men having underwear with metal wire and padding that fitted tightly around their balls to make their packages look more attractive to women? Can you imagine them putting up with a contraption that made them sigh with relief when they took it off at night?

If you can, try not to always wear a bra, especially ones that have underwiring as we don't want such a conductive material constantly near our breasts. Your bra should never leave a mark on your body when you take it off. If it does, this shows it's too tight and will be constricting the very important lymph cells. This means that lymph fluid which helps take bacteria, viruses, cellular debris, cancer cells, and toxins away from the breasts will not be able to flow freely and drain from this area, which we need to keep our breasts in health. We need the lymph fluid around our breasts to flow freely for optimal breast health. If you have to wear a bra for comfort or convenience and it can't be a soft bralette or something else that doesn't tighten around your breast area, then take your bra off as soon as you can each day and give yourself a lovely boob massage to boost the circulation in that area. I'm sure that's the reason women love to take their bras off and why it feels so good – your breasts know they're not meant to be pushed up, dug into and suffocated all day, every day. Free your boobs!

It's time to reclaim your breasts and realise that there's no one way they're meant to look throughout your lifetime. Also try not to berate or criticise your breasts as they age. If your nipples start to point downwards instead of sticking out in front and pointing at others, then take it as a sign it's now time to be more pleasing and sexy for yourself not others. If your breasts have shrunk, changed through childbirth, or been removed by surgery, then use this as a reminder that your role is no longer to please and 'nurture' the rest of the world before yourself. It's time to start feeding *your* desires, nourishing *your* true self, and nurturing *your* dreams to reality.

Do make sure you check your breasts for any unusual lumps, bumps, or nipple puckering/discharge. If anything has changed or doesn't seem normal, then pop over to your GP and get it checked out.

**Tummy**

Until a few years ago, I didn't realise that you're not only "allowed" to have a rounded tummy but that you're biologically meant to. As a woman, even the "flattest" tummy will have a curve because it's designed to protect your precious womb and other internal organs in that area.

Women have been shamed into hating their tummies and calling them mum tums, jelly bellies, saggy, stretched, gross or un-toned. Your tummy isn't any of those things. It's just your tummy, which like everything else in life will sometimes be bigger than other people's and sometimes smaller. Sometimes it'll be smooth, other times it'll have ripples, scars, texture, and marks. Sometimes you'll see muscles, other times rolls. NONE OF THESE ARE WRONG.

I had a flat-ish tummy in my 20s and I wasn't happy with myself at all. In my 30s, I got so bored of hating myself and being mean to parts of my body that I just started to stop. Not overnight, but day by day, the unlearning continued and I decided to like, not loathe, myself. I hung out with women who were comfortable in their own skin and limited my time spent with diet-obsessed ones. I learnt that there's no shape or size your tummy should be and, because you're a living organism, you're allowed to change over the years. The aim of loving your tum (and hopefully the rest of you) isn't to stop being good to yourself with nourishing food and movement – because both of the things are essential for your health and sparkle. It's so you start to relax and realise that your body is not a static thing that needs to be frozen in time and that it has a natural shape and curve, that's not wrong.

My tummy goes up in size in winter, when I'm on my period, and when I slouch. It goes down when I stand up straight, when I'm ovulating, when it's spring and summer, and when I'm super busy. I'm in my 40's now and my tummy is much rounder than it was ten years ago. But hey, so are most men's around me so why can't my tummy change shape without it being a big deal? I've also seen that there's a crucial link to the fact that women have been trained to always "breathe in" to hold their tummies in and not speaking up or out. The more women focus on impossible beauty standards, like having a flat tummy, the less likely they'll be able to speak out about issues of justice and inequality around them. So, think about speaking out more in this life more than you do sucking your tummy in.

We often look back at Victorian women who wore corsets to be the 'ideal shape', frequently fainted and suffered internal injuries due to the unnatural shape they were being forced into and think they were silly women. However, much of the clothes and fashion of today is still trying to get women to suck their stomachs in (just like a corset did) and can squash our precious womb area. Super tight clothing, suck-in pants that dig into our stomachs, or anything we have to breathe in to wear or feels uncomfortable, is no less oppressive to women than those whalebone corsets tightly laced all those years ago.

I don't want to spend the next 40 years of my life trying to have a flat tummy, it's as futile and time consuming (for most women) as trying to have a flat forehead. I have too many other things I want to do with my life. My husband doesn't breathe in when he's sat on a sun lounger, so why should I? Beautiful fabrics ripple, roll, and crumple when they're folded over, so why can't my tummy? I want to be vibrant, eat foods that makes me glow and move my body to boost my mental and physical health. But, I don't want to try for a lifetime to get a flat tummy and focus on that more than my purpose and passions – as I did for many years.

Your tummy will go up and down in different seasons and for different reasons – childbirth, illness, different stages of your menstrual cycle, and that's all normal. If you're suffering from uncomfortable bloating from things like fibroids, IBS, excess weight in that area that makes you feel incredibly uncomfortable then please seek out some help for those things. There's a difference between knowing you don't need a six-pack and ignoring your health in this area.

It's time to concentrate on doing things that give you butterflies in your tummy or make you laugh until your belly aches, not waste time worrying about the size or shape of it. Let your tummy, like your bum, knee or elbow, have a natural curve to it. Let your womb expand and contract over your cycle and don't let anyone shame you into thinking it's wrong. If your tummy hangs down after childbirth or a procedure, let this be your medal for creating life or surviving – this fleshy medal just so happens to hang around your tummy instead of your neck.

Again, if a flat-ish tummy is your natural shape or the natural consequence of your lifestyle and activities then great, but if not, stop putting off going swimming, going to the beach, or feeling at home in your one, precious body.

One of the best books you'll ever read on body image and how you can super-boost yours is *Body Positive Power: Because life is already happening and you don't need flat abs to live it* by Meghan Jayne Crabbe. This is one of the books I recommend most to my clients and I'd love for you to read it too because I think it's genuinely life-changing. And instead of you thinking your tummy is one of the reasons you're unlovable, it'll put a fire in your belly to love yourself more.

## Thighs

My thighs were always one of my most "problem" areas. It seemed that no matter how much exercise I did, or stupid diets I tried, they always stayed larger than what my obsessive magazine reading told me was "normal" or attractive. In my twenties I used to be a choreographer for music videos. I was once choreographing a music video shoot at a pool with about ten super skinny models in bikinis. Suddenly, the director came up to me and asked, "Can you dive?" Without thinking, I said, "Yes" and before I knew it, I was put in a swimsuit and told to stand next to the line of models.

I was dying inside. All I could do was look at my thighs, which moved in places that theirs didn't and nestled into each other where theirs had a gap. Mine showed cellulite when the sun hit them and theirs didn't (or so I thought). One of the models was 14! Basically a child! I was 24, and even with my supposed older wisdom, I was still comparing my body to a teenager's. I hated myself that day. I felt so self-conscious and ashamed. But guess what, when the music video aired, I hadn't been edited out because I was a grotesque lump of lard like I'd told myself. I'd actually been given a leading role in the video and my thighs (and diving skills) looked pretty darn fine. Yes, they were different from the 6ft or 14-year-old models, yes they moved and swished as I walked, but that's all they were – different, not a disaster. 15 years on from that music video, my thighs nestle together even more snugly and have more cellulite, but I don't care about it like I did then. I want a life full of energy and sparkle, and I got tired of caring if my thighs were supposedly the wrong shape, size, or texture.

Also, let's just take a little moment to talk about cellulite because too many women (myself included) have struggled, or are still struggling with the heavily advertised notion that it's a flaw, not a flourish, of nature. Too many women aren't wearing the clothes they want or enjoying their bodies in the sunshine because they feel ashamed after being told for decades that cellulite is a defect not design of nature. Well, I say ballbags to that!

Speaking of ballbags – men have textured skin on theirs. Yet they're not being sold expensive creams and treatments. Okay, so a treatment called 'Scrotox' was attempted, but just like the male pill, the majority of men weren't up for having sensitive areas of their bodies injected or altered. The majority of that sort of stuff is reserved for women it seems. So, it's about time we stood up for our cellulite and stop believing it must be eradicated. The majority of women have cellulite. Babies have it. Supermodels have it, movie stars have it. Yet, the trouble is, like the 'sparkle lines' on our faces, it gets airbrushed out of pictures. We're not told about this consistent airbrushing! So we grow up feeling alone and like it's only our body that's not up to this fake, photoshopped standard.

Do you realise this airbrushing of women in magazines, videos or through phone filters – be it wrinkles, pores, or cellulite, is actually censorship. Women's true bodies and textures have been censored as it's deemed wrong. This has given generations of women the most warped idea of what's normal. Cellulite is normal. I'd love you to no longer point it out, grimace, or call your skin texture 'gross'. I'd love us women to reclaim that name and follow the example of the gorgeous actor Tabitha Brown (@iamtabithabrown) who calls it CELLuLIGHT and says it's "simply light trying to push through my cells." I love this! Let's run our fingers over that texture and be interested in the sheer art of it – the same way we would the texture on a beautiful shell. Let's always see it as light and sparkle pushing through our cells to display itself in the world.

Let's also start demanding to see cellulite in pictures, on TV or in movies so it becomes normal for the girls growing up behind us to not think it's the shameful flaw we've been brainwashed to believe. Let's get other women to join us in showing our thighs and form a 'cell-u-light crew' or 'babe bumps bunch' and give ourselves permission to wear shorts or swimwear without feeling shame (if you're on Instagram then go follow @steviebstylefashion, @stylemesunday @danaemercer and @thebirdspapaya who will encourage and uplift you about having texture on your body). Look around you today – where do you see texture? Look at different foods, objects, animals, and landscapes and marvel at the divine art of those designs. The more you see lines and texture as beautiful on trees, shells, and mountains, the more you'll see the beauty of it on your human body. Touch the texture on your body and say something loving to it.

Start taking care of those fabulous thighs of yours. Slather them in moisturiser. Thank them for holding up your body and concentrate on the fact they're waiting to take you dancing, roller-skating, and to all the places you want to go to in your one and only sparkle-filled life.

## Lower Legs

When I was on holiday last year, I put sun cream on one of my lower legs and gasped. It seemed that overnight another broken vein had appeared – bright purple and blue and highly visible due to the contrast of my pale legs. "Great, another blemish!" was my automatic thought. "Another mark that I

317

have to think about covering up or getting removed" was the next thought. And then I remembered – I've been taught to panic when my body produces colour or texture that's not shown in pictures or ideas of alleged female perfection. I've been trained as a woman and consumer to think about who I can give my money to for a procedure so my body can look "acceptable" and airbrushed. I was actually shocked at my ingrained knee-jerk reaction to this new artistic addition on my lower leg. I reminded myself that skin isn't meant to be mark, mole or vein free. It's not meant to be one uniformed colour and texture like a plastic mannequin.

Only the week before discovering this new addition on my leg, I'd been marveling at an artist's work (check out lillymaidesigns.weebly.com or @lillymaidesigns on Instagram) who uses the most beautiful colours, often layering, mixing and swirling them together in a mesmerising, marble effect. So, I reminded myself of this beautiful art that I'd been captivated by and took another look at my shin. I realised what I'd initially panicked was wrong or unsightly actually, looked like a part of the paintings I'd been in awe of – purples, pinks, and blues all swirled together on the pale canvas of my leg.

So, this is just to tell you that your lower legs aren't too pale or dark. They don't have too many veins or moles or freckles. It doesn't matter if your skin isn't all one colour. It doesn't matter if your ankles are the same width as your calves.

It doesn't matter if they're skinny or wide. Your lower legs are wonderful. Wear the skirts or shorts if you want to. Stop believing they're meant to be a boring blank canvas when they're a beautiful, texture, and colour-filled work of art.

*NB. Of course if you notice a mole that's changed in size, appearance, or texture or a new red or pink mark/spot appears on your lower leg, then please go get it checked out by your GP.*

## Bum

Guess what? Your bum isn't the wrong shape, size, or texture either — are you kind of getting the message about all your body parts now? Your bum isn't too big, small, droopy, or flat. It's allowed to change and grow, and it can be as smooth as a peach or textured as a pineapple. It's your sparkle seat! It's your dancing partner and it deserves more love. There's absolutely nothing wrong with exercising and strengthening certain parts of your body or going to the gym. That's all fab and will boost your mental and physical health. However, there's a reason your bum is behind you — it's because you're meant to ignore it, not think you constantly need to sculpt it, shrink it, or surgically alter it. Let it just get on with doing its job while you keep looking ahead, walking towards your happiest life, enjoying yourself, and shaking it to music that makes you sparkle. What's your favourite bum-shaking tune? Go play that in the next 24 hours, sing your heart out and shake your sparkly booty to it.

## Vulva

Can you point to your vulva? Maybe you call it your vagina, lady parts, pussy, or sparkle flaps?! So many of us were never taught the correct name. Your vulva is the whole of the external part of your genitals, including the outer and inner lips (or labia). Your vagina is the part of your anatomy that connects your uterus to the outside world; the canal where a penis goes during sex and where your menstrual blood and babies come out of. If someone was talking about your foot and kept calling it an ankle, you'd want to correct them. Let's correct any person who says "vagina" and doesn't mean the inner part of our female reproductive anatomy. Like the lack of knowledge around a woman's menstrual cycle and clitoris, the lack of understanding of what constitutes a vagina and vulva keeps women's bodies in a place of being less important and respected than men's and even shameful.

Sadly, once again, due to the explosion of the porn industry, women (from an increasingly young age) have been taught that their intimate parts should look teenage or childlike. Have you realised that often we don't even question this creepy ideal? We've just believed this powerful messaging, drip-fed to us, telling us that there's only one sexual ideal and if your vulva looks different, you need to wax it, laser it, or go under the knife to change it? It's actually shocking when you think about it. Because of this negative and pervasive messaging, you probably believe that your vulva doesn't look good and perhaps isn't feminine, sexy, and attractive – not true! Vulvas are as varied as flowers in a garden. All unique, all beautiful.

And what about pubes? Well, unless you (not porn, pop culture, or your partner) prefer your vulva without any hair, just save yourself some money and consider letting them grow. Pubic hair and how it looks is a personal choice but, know that they do have a reason for adorning your vulva. Like eyelashes protect your eyes, pubic hair helps prevent bacteria and other pathogens entering your vagina. I'd go for some protective pubes over vaginal infections any day, but that's just me.

Also, why is it that hair in different areas of our body is either allowed or not for women? It's allowed on our head and eyes – in fact we're even encouraged to add more hair onto those areas and pay for extensions to be more attractive AND to be seen as desirable. We're most certainly not allowed as women to have it on our legs, underarms, or vulvas and should regularly pay to have it removed. Not suggesting any hair removal revolutions just yet, just interesting to note the 'beauty police' that women obey without even realising the unwritten laws for our bodies. It also makes me realise why men have more of the world's wealth when their beauty standards and amount of body parts they're encouraged to "fix" are far less.

## Your Dream Body

There you have it. Time to stop obsessing over the many parts of your body and know that they're as unique as your fingerprints and, as with everything, over time they'll change. The "perfect" body is like a unicorn – it may be promoted as a cute idea, but it doesn't actually exist.

It's not your fault if you hate the way you look because for years you've been presented with endless images of women without softness, stretchmarks, wrinkles, cell-u-light, or breasts that droop. This censorship of women's bodies has been so intense it's caused women to look at their own bodies – be it varicose veins, long inner labia, or different sized boobs – and think they're inherently wrong. It's caused shame and silence, and stopped the celebration of life and a body that can help you achieve and do all you're meant to. Just in the same way we're incensed when we hear about countries censoring the internet or certain news stories, we should feel the same anger that as women we've had the real variety of women's bodies kept from us and then told we must spend money to alter ourselves to be acceptable or attractive.

You need to realise you and I have been cheated out of both money and years of enjoying our bodies and lives. Isn't it time to call out the madness of having your body dissected and dishonoured and take your power and sparkle back? Start to move away from thinking your body is a total mess and begin to marvel at it. You won't undo a lifetime's programming overnight, but, day by day, it can happen. Once you start saying good things to yourself and realising there are people and companies who need to make you feel insecure to keep them rich, you can claim back both your money and body. You'll soon realise you're not an ongoing renovation project. Your body is an instrument, not an ornament. If you have dreams you want to reach in this lifetime and a body that can help you get there – then you have a dream body!

**Sparkle school homework** – Is there a part of your body you want to stop hating so much and instead of being cruel to it, could now say something kind, wonderful or even apologise to it? If there is, touch that part now. Marvel at its texture, colour, abilities and appearance and say something that'll fill it with sparkle, not shame.

## Lesson 3

**UNLEARN: Women aren't like dogs.**

Feel free to call me a dog. I'm serious. I know it's traditionally been used as a put down for women, but I take it as one of the highest compliments because 1) I adore dogs and 2) I believe women *are* like dogs.

Let me tell you about my dog. She has short legs, a big fluffy bum that waddles when she walks, wrinkles on her face, a broad chest and she doesn't look like any of the other dogs you see on TV or when we go out for a walk. My dog's so comfortable in her own skin, she actually struts. My dog loves going to the park. She's outside, there's grass under her feet, she can walk around (she's not much of a runner), she loves to sniff everything or lie down, relax and watch the world go by. She's surrounded by the most vivacious, varied dogs all enjoying themselves, too. She doesn't dread going to the dog park because there may be slimmer, taller, or allegedly better-looking dogs than her.

If a Great Dane bounds over to my dog, she doesn't think, "Urgh, I don't want that dog to stand next to me because my legs look stumpy next to hers." She doesn't see a little Dachshund and think, "Oh my God, I'm so fat. I need to lose weight because that other dog is so cute and little."

Similarly, other dogs don't see my dog and think, "Look at her tail, it curls and mine is straight. I need to get an operation so I can have a curly tail like hers!" No, these dogs just live their lives and interact together without comparison or self-hatred. They exist side-by-side knowing that another dog's appearance has no bearing on their own worth. It's made me realise *this* is how we're meant to feel as women when we're around or see other women.

My dog will never look like a Labrador. If my dog had been brainwashed over her lifetime by seeing media images that urged her to look like a Labrador, then she'd need to have her legs stretched, fur cut and dyed, and extensive surgery on her face to lengthen her nose. If we saw a dog go through these serious operations to look like another dog, we'd think it was sad and cruel. We'd probably even go so far as to call it inhumane.

However, with women, we've been trained to think it's totally normal or okay to do everything necessary to try and look like an entirely different "breed" of woman. Cutting ourselves up, injecting our skin, and doing all sorts of other things to look different has been normalised. If it's not alright for us to do that to dogs, cats, or any other animal, then in my mind it shouldn't be normal for women. You own your body and you can do whatever you want with it, especially if it genuinely gives you more sparkle and sass. But, if the aim is to look like an entirely different woman because you've been systematically taught you're not good enough or worthy as you are, then surgery won't address the root issue.

Dogs are all different breeds. Some tall, some short, some stocky, some with short hair, some with long hair, some athletic, some muscly, some skinny – and neither the dog nor their owners think they're wrong. As women, however, we've been taught to think that variety within our species is wrong. We've never been taught we're actually like dogs and are different breeds, determined by our genes. My "breed" is short and curvy with round cheeks, cell-u-light on my thighs, blue eyes, white skin, and a round bottom. That's just my "breed." I'll never have long legs, red hair, black skin, or big round boobs, but it's wonderful that other women do. You weren't created to spend your life looking at other women and thinking, "I should look like her." No, just like my dog, you're meant to focus on enjoying your life, being your own beautiful breed and knowing that no one breed is better than another. In fact, the world is a better more interesting place because there are so many different breeds.

A healthy size and weight for a dog isn't determined by it just being a dog and having to look like the most desirable dog – it's determined by its breed. A size and weight that's perfect for one breed could for another breed be overweight or underweight and affect its function to live a happy, healthy life. My dog weighs 32kg – which would be overweight and cause health problems for a Chihuahua, but would be underweight for an adult St. Bernard. My dog gets weighed if she ever goes to the vets, but I don't put her on the scales every day to see if she's gained or lost a pound. I just feed her the type and amount of food that's perfect for her breed, let her enjoy some yummy treats too, and make sure her cute body gets all the movement it needs to be happy and healthy.

Even though there may be a size or shape you want to be as a woman, it's your breed (i.e. your natural size and shape) that will dictate the size you're healthiest at. Anything grossly under or over that weight range (yes, you're meant to have a healthy weight range as a woman, NOT a static number to aim for) can affect your health and happiness. I sometimes have clients who want to lose weight but it's clear they're already underweight for their "breed". I ask them, "If you didn't overeat or under eat, or over exercise or under exercise – what size do you think your body would naturally be?" – and the answers are astounding.

There's not one woman who doesn't know the size and shape her body's naturally meant to be (sometimes it's more than she currently weighs, sometimes it's less, and sometimes she has to admit that even though she wants to lose weight, she's the size she should be). The pain and problem comes when that size or shape doesn't fit in with the size and shape a woman has been told she has to be to look healthy or attractive – which again is utter BS. Women can be healthy, happy, and attractive – just like dogs – whatever their natural size and shape is. It took me a long time to accept my breed. I've been underweight from constant dieting and overweight when I got ill and both these states dampened my health and sparkle – just as it would a dog's.

If I hadn't grasped this fact – that I'm my own breed of woman – then I would've had a severe anxiety attack when I found out one day that part of my husband's new job was to fly across the world and interview a Victoria's Secret model. Talk about a test from the universe! The negative voices in my head had a field day, telling me that once my husband met this "perfect" woman, he'd think coming back to me was a downgrade. So, I dug deep into the truth that 1) I too am a total one-off miracle and the media has just tried to tell me that only a certain type of woman is perfection, and 2) my husband was just off to meet a different breed of woman. When he walks our dog, he doesn't suddenly decide that our cute, fluffy pooch isn't good enough and ditch her for another dog. So, why should I believe that I'm any different or less loved than our dog?

As I waved him off to meet this other breed of woman, I didn't dress up or parade around in heels and angel wings. Nope, I gave him a hug in my onesie with spot cream on, knowing that he was lucky to have me. If you'd have told me a decade ago that I'd confidently say goodbye to my partner whilst he went to meet a supermodel and not lose sleep (or try and lose a ton of weight) in his absence, I would've said you were crazy. But now I realise the *really* crazy thing is believing we should all look like one breed of media-championed woman. I refuse to buy into the insulting narrative that a partner only stays with a woman because they've not met or been seduced by someone more attractive. No way! Our worth is so much greater than that ladies!

So, go hang out in a dog park – look at all the crazy and wonderful breeds of dogs and then go to a beach or park and enjoy looking at the crazy and wonderful breeds of women. And then be like my dog. Just be you. Sleep, eat, enjoy your food, drink water, get out in nature, make friends with new people and don't compare yourself to your fellow gorgeous creatures – even the ones with long legs and angel wings. Your body and face are gifts never to be replicated in the entire history of the universe. And if you ever want to try and look like someone else, you must remember that you my darling are high-end couture – not a counterfeit.

**Sparkle school homework** – Have some fun with this one. Which breed of dog do you think you're most like? What are the cutest and coolest elements about that breed? Does it have a big nose, chunky legs, a slim body or lots of hair? Now, what are 3 wonderful traits of your "breed" of woman? Do you have long legs, a curvy bottom, big feet or curly hair? Write them down and realise that your breed makes you special and lovable and no other breed is better (or worse) than yours.

**Lesson 4**

**UNLEARN: Weighing your worth**

I ask most of my clients how often they weigh themselves. Not because I'm nosy but because I know it'll 100% impact their sparkle. Most screw their faces up and sheepishly say, "Every day. That's bad isn't it?" Well no, it's not bad because you're not bad, but it's not helpful, either. In fact, it'll spoil your sparkle and is generally as useful an indicator of your health as counting your eyelashes every day.

I weighed myself religiously for nearly 20 years – from when I was a teenager to around 35. It started because I grew up being taught that's what women did. That's what my mum did and that's what other mums did. That's what my sister did, and the girls at school, and that's what the women on TV and in magazines did. I grew up in the era where women went to slimming clubs every week to be weighed and were forever trying new diets involving grapefruits, cabbages, shakes, or counting points. I grew up learning that part of being a woman was obsessing over your weight. You *had* to know what your weight was to know if your body was good or bad, attractive or a disappointment.

I was utterly obsessed with my weight. The number produced on that square, metal box ruled my life. I felt like a better, more valuable, more attractive, worthy woman if that number was the one I wanted to see. If it was over the number I wanted to see, then I felt everything from shame and self-hatred to deep disappointment and utter disgust. That number affected me and my feelings of worth so much, it would dictate if I would actually go to parties and see people or not. How sad a number made me feel like that and I actually missed out on spending time with friends because I felt I was the wrong "number"? What I didn't realise was that I wasn't actually weighing my body. I was weighing my worth as a woman. The higher the number on the scales, the lower my worth and vice versa.

If you've grown up weighing yourself and still constantly do, you're likely measuring your worth as a woman and not your waistline, too. You've been taught religiously that you need to know what you weigh for health reasons, but I'm telling you (unless you suffer with excess weight that impairs your breathing, movement, and ability to live) obsessing about the number on the scale has little bearing on your physical

331

health. It does a great deal of damage to your mental health and sparkle though.

Weight loss companies and the diet industry urges women to get on the scales daily or weekly. This isn't how you were meant to live and just like those fairground games that are rigged from the start, you can't win the weighing game. This is because without understanding how your female body works in a monthly cycle and how certain foods and exercise regimes react differently in women than in men, "winning" the weighing game is a lifelong pursuit. Your weight was never meant to be constantly measured or static. You were never meant to have a "target weight" that you try and stick to every day for the rest of your life. Your weight isn't even meant to be a thing because like the number of hairs on your head, it fluctuates daily, weekly, and monthly.

Your female hormones mean that your body changes and holds onto weight at different times of the month or your life. And just as the tide of the sea goes in and out, your waist/thighs/bum/boobs will all go in and out depending on your cycle and season of life. At sometimes of the year, like when it's colder, your body will often hold onto more weight to stay warm and protect your organs and, at other times of the year, it'll naturally hold onto less weight. This is just what a woman's body living in a natural world does.

There are no longer any scales in my house to dictate my worth. I haven't weighed myself in over five years which means *I* get to decide if I feel good about my body. I now go to parties not knowing how much I weigh because it's irrelevant and a random number (one that would change if I drank a glass of water or went for a poo) doesn't get to decide my social worth anymore.

Lots of clients come to me with 'weight loss' as one of their biggest goals to achieve a sparkle-filled life. I never allow this as a primary goal, though, because I know it's not really the thing a woman wants – it's only what she's been *taught* to want. When I dig a little deeper, every woman's true desire isn't to hit her "target weight", it's actually to feel more confident, energised, sexy, happy, vibrant and yes, often lighter. However, that's just as much an emotional thing as it is physical.

Instead of your "target weight", try and think about your "target feeling" that you want to reach. If you focus on the things that make your whole life sparkle – nourishing food, movement, pleasure, fun, speaking-up for your needs, and reducing inflammation, then you should naturally reach your "target feeling". If you have excess weight to lose and it's affecting your health, confidence or stopping you sparkling, then balancing your hormones and pursuing your sparkle (with the above things) should naturally achieve that. Please don't let an inanimate object like a set of scales or fluctuating number

333

affect your worth as a woman. By all means get help or support to be inspired with your food and lifestyle choices so that you can feel your very best, but don't place your happiness, health, and sparkle in the hands of a number.

You have more knowledge of your body than a box with numbers. You know if you feel good or bad, healthy, or unhealthy, vibrant, or sluggish. You'll know if you feel heavier or if you've lost weight for no reason and should be concerned. You know this by tuning into how you feel, how you look, and how your clothes fit. Also, don't forget clothing sizes change from brand to brand and were never meant to be a thing (clothes were always meant to be made to fit us, not the other way round). I have everything in my wardrobe from a size 8 to size 18, and those numbers don't mean a thing. There's no standardisation of clothing sizes, which is beyond crazy – can you imagine if there was no standardisation of speed limits and different cars speedometer's interpreted the numbers differently? That would be physically dangerous. You thinking you should only fit into a certain size of clothes, regardless of the fact in a different shop it would be a different number, is mentally dangerous. So, just buy whatever clothes you love and feel fab in because the number or letter inside of them is truly irrelevant.

**Sparkle school homework** – I want you to seriously think about breaking up with your scales. Can you throw them away, hide them or put a note covering the numbers that just says, "Stop weighing your worth, you're wonderful"?

## Lesson 5

**UNLEARN: You have to stop nature.**

Everything on this earth ages as time passes. We start ageing from the moment we're born. We're not meant to age prematurely through too much stress, sugar, and other inflammatory things. Nonetheless, we're meant to age. Yet the unrelenting message you receive as a woman is that you're meant to stay physically suspended in time from about the age of 25. You're expected to spend your hard-earned money and precious time (that you could be having all sorts of fun with) trying to stop yourself from ageing. Every day you're bombarded with messages (usually from companies wanting to make lots of money from your insecurities) telling you that as a woman you should do all you can to stop any signs of the passing of time being shown on your body. As far as I know, no scientist or earthly genius has been able to stop time yet, so why should women be tasked with committing their lives to this unnatural cause? Do you realise how exhausting it is to try and hold back the passing of time!

If you were a teenage girl in the 1990s like me, you would've been encouraged by the media to get a padded, push-up bra ("Hello boys"), put on make-up, and dress sexily so that you looked older? And then what happens? You get older and you're urged by the media and images all around you to have the skin, body, and face of – yep, you guessed it – a teenager. I think that's the actual definition of a head f**k and a way to totally sabotage your sparkle.

Throughout your whole life as a woman, you've received the overt or covert message that beauty and looking young should be a priority for you. It should come before or at least run parallel to your dreams, goals, and the enjoyment of your life. You've been encouraged from a variety of industries and the media to spend your money on the latest cream, lotion, and potion, or start injecting or cutting up your "flawed" body. Why? Because the silent law that many women have been duped into living by from their 30's onwards is: "Thou shalt not age."

Day by day, you can see that the anti-ageing brainwashing is being ramped up and taught to girls at a younger and younger age. We're being shown more and more pictures of line-free, texture-less, expression-less, pouty, perky female faces and bodies. Women are taught that they cannot show up as they are – they have to hide their age or pores or sparkle lines with creams, make-up, and filters for photos.

We're being encouraged to strive to look like a life-less, crease-less fem-bot, instead of a living, breathing, textured and sparkle-filled sass-pot. It's no wonder then that given this unrealistic expectation women feel worn out, upset, depleted, defeated, detached from and unable to enjoy their miraculous bodies on a daily basis.

Do you know the energy it takes to do all of your day-to-day stuff *and* live against the flow of nature by buying, trying, or hoping to not visibly age? It's literally like telling a tree to bloom in spring and summer but that it can't lose any of its leaves in autumn or winter – and if it does – it needs to spend all its time and money sticking them back on instead of enjoying (and finding the beauty in) each season of its life. You weren't meant to live your life trying to defy nature and stick all your leaves back on. You're not meant to look like a teenager. You don't exist just to constantly look young or sexually pleasing to men. You're not meant to try and stop time – you're meant to enjoy your time.

Wanting to look 10 or 20 years younger isn't the biggest dream you should have for your life – even though we've been sold that it is and so many of us have just not questioned it. I know it's tough. It's still a daily unlearning process for me too, but let's be pro healthy, sparkly ageing not anti-ageing. Let's start spreading the message that we don't want to look a decade or generation younger. We wouldn't applaud a 10-year-old who wanted to look a decade younger and have the face and body of a new-born baby – that would be horrible. We'd think it utterly strange if a 20-year-old had extensive surgery to look like a 10-year-old because that would be weird. So, let's take the same view that it shouldn't be considered the norm for any woman over 35 to always try and look 10 years younger.

Stars in the sky don't track their age. They just shine brightly and fulfil their purpose until it's their time to leave the universe. Women are meant to do the same. Refuse to let your age affect or limit your life because then you'll increase your sparkle and natural youthfulness. Youthfulness, btw, is a wonderful thing that you can possess as a woman until the day you die. Being youthful doesn't mean looking eternally young. It means having an energy and vivaciousness that comes from pursuing your passions and dreams and caring for the health of your body. It's about being YOU-TO-THE-FULL – no cream or procedure can give you the youthful glow that being you-to-the-full can!

Your body is going to change – just as any living thing does, but let's not see this change as negative. I love following Sarah Nicole Laundry on Instagram @thebirdspapaya as she's always showing the beauty of the changes in her body. She doesn't buy into the BS that your body should "bounce back" after a baby or life-changing situation. She says that our bodies "bounce forward" and I love that.

So, lavish yourself with good food, movement, self-care, and indulge in any beauty or sparkle-boosting treatments that make you feel fabulous and glow – why not? Enjoy being the best version of *you* at every age. Just think about perhaps refusing to commit so much time, focus, and energy trying to stop nature from taking its course. Instead, focus on being an unstoppable force of nature!

**Sparkle school homework** – I want you to think of an outfit, person, type of music and activity that makes you feel most youthful. I want you to think about including each of these in your life over the next few weeks and seeing how it can make you feel more YOU-TO-THE-FULL.

## Lesson 6

### UNLEARN: Your style is superficial.

I used to think that getting my sparkle back could only be done through deep emotional and spiritual work. When I lived abroad in my early 30's, I was at one of the lowest times in my life. I was ill and lonely, and struggling mentally and physically. I thought I needed to delve deep into the dark places I was struggling with to find my way back to the light. I thought I needed to read more, learn more, pray more, rest more, believe more, hope more, and talk it out more. I knew that time was a healer, but I felt I'd been without my sparkle for so long that time just seemed to taunt me – it was like I was in prison with no idea how long my sentence was. I was always waiting to wake up and hopefully one day feel like myself again. But, one morning as I looked in the mirror and saw myself in another shapeless, drab top with leggings, unwashed hair and face with no make-up, I suddenly had a brainwave. "Perhaps you need to *look* like the best version of yourself again to *feel* like the best version of yourself again!?" Could something so superficial actually be divine inspiration?

So, I showered, washed my hair, took time over my make-up, and pulled something out of my closet that made me feel fab and not frumpy. And I felt better. Not just a little bit better. I felt quite a lot better about myself. Better than I had done in a long time. I "saw" myself for the first time in what'd felt like forever. It actually shocked me that maybe, just maybe, the sparkly version of me hadn't disappeared entirely. Even though there was still sadness and struggle on the inside of me – a brighter and happier outside really did boost my sparkle more than all of the deep spiritual work I'd been trying and failing at for months.

This small act of showering, doing my hair and make-up, and dressing in something lovely gave me back a sense of power and pleasure. It made me feel that, if nothing else in my circumstances changed, if no big breakthroughs occurred, then there was something I could do to make myself feel a little better. This focus of my appearance wasn't superficial or worthless. This was deeply spiritual and one of the keys to kick-starting my sparkle again.

At least once a week, I started to "sparkle up" and dress the way I wanted to feel again – happy, joyful, sassy, sexy, and fashionable, not how I currently felt and was dressing – depressed and dowdy. However, the sadness I was feeling, the financial problems we were experiencing, the painful eczema I was suffering with, the career blocks I was facing, couldn't be eased by just dressing nicely, could they? Well, no, it didn't take away all the tough stuff, but it did start to shift some of the heaviness that I'd been carrying during that time. It did make a parting in the dense fog of my days. Dressing like the best and happiest version of myself (even when I felt far from that) started to become a regular thing and always lifted my spirits. This tiny boost in my confidence would often give me just enough energy and 'oomph' to do at least one other positive thing for myself that day.

So, I created #SparkleUpThursday. First of all, it was just for me. Then when I joined Instagram, it became for the women who followed me. Every Thursday, we'd all "sparkle-up" and have a day, or even an hour, where we asked ourselves,

"What would make me feel less crappy and more sparkly?" For some it was wearing sequins, their favourite earrings, or brightest lipstick. For others it was washing their hair, taking extra time with their make-up, or wearing their best shoes to unload the dishwasher. And while I no longer do it as a weekly call to action on Instagram, many women have still carried on the #SparkleUpThursday tradition which makes my heart sing.

So, why not once a week "sparkle up" and decide to wear and look exactly how you want to feel? Just start wearing things more regularly that put a spring in your step and sparkle in your eyes. I don't know why putting the bins out in a party dress feels better than when I do it in my pajamas, but it just does! Sometimes I even wear a crown to make my morning cuppa because it reminds me that even if a list of tasks for others awaits me, I'm still a Queen. The gorgeous sparkle-filled Karen Arthur on Instagram (@thekarenarthur) is a big fan of women using fashion to boost their mood and day, and encourages women to #wearyourhappy, which I love, so you should check her out.

In the same way your body will tell you which foods make you feel great and boost your energy, the same is true for clothes. If you put something on and you feel better, more energised, or more like you – then that's for you. If you feel drab, dowdy, or uncomfortable, then even if the world's top stylist tells you that you look "fabulous, daaaarling", don't you

342

dare believe them. Dress like a woman with sparkle even when you don't feel like one – or try and do it at least once or twice a week to help get your sparkle back because it certainly helped me.

**Sparkle school homework** – If you're at home right now and not wearing one single thing that you like or feel nice in, go add or change something about it, so you do.   You might swap your stained sweater for a sequin top. You might add some lippy or your favourite earrings. You might just go put on your favourite shoes (that you can no longer walk in) to have your cup of tea. You might put on your best pj's instead of your grubby ones. Just go put on anything that makes you feel a little more like how you want to feel, regardless of how you currently feel.

**1 small sparkly step for today (because you've already done a lot of homework)…**

1) This is some of the most important sparkle homework you'll ever do. It's time to re-inhabit your body, not stay disconnected with it through constant criticism and fault-finding. Go to the mirror, and despite every negative thought or comment that may appear in your head, smile at yourself and say one positive thing about your appearance. Next, touch a line, scar, piece of

textured skin or area that's changed from what it used to be. Tell that area why it's full of beauty and not full of shame – even if you don't believe it at this point. Do it as if you were speaking to a child or your best friend – because that's what your body is to you – both a child that deserves to be loved and a best friend who's gone through so much with you. I want you to do these two things every day for the next month and I promise you'll see and feel a change in your body. Your body will respond to being loved, not loathed. Day by day you'll increase your glow and enjoy watching your sparkle grow!

# FINAL SPARKLY

# SENTIMENT

*"You wander from room to room, hunting for the diamond necklace, that is already around your neck."*

Rumi

I want to tell you one important thing before you reach the end of this book...

You didn't need to get your sparkle back. You only needed to return to it. Your entire body is actually made up of remnants of stars from huge explosions that happened in the galaxies – that's a scientific fact, not a poetic description. The sparkle of stars resides in all your cells – you're literally, not metaphorically, a woman with sparkle. You're a wonder of nature. A light-filled being. A living work or art. A one-off never to be repeated in the whole of history. Yes, you.

Despite any darkness or despair you might have felt or still feel, your sparkle and true self will always be there. This idea is again backed up by scientists who've discovered that what we see with our eyes as complete darkness isn't. Slivers of light, called 'neutrinos', are always present, even if we can't see them. The same is true of your sparkle – even when you believe it's been dampened, dulled, or totally covered by the rubble of life's 'earthquakes' – it's still there. If you feel there's only grey or darkness surrounding you – I promise you, there's sparkle there. Just like those slivers of light invisible to the naked eye, your true self and sparkle are ever present.

I want you to take this knowledge – that you're a woman filled with sparkle – and start speaking the truth of who you are and what you want from this one precious life of yours. Start obsessing over your dreams the way you've been obsessing over your body. Start dancing to your own tune instead of the constant demands of others. Surround yourself with people who encourage you and make your heart so happy it could burst. Get into the flow of your female cycle and the seasons. Speak up for yourself. Find more things that make you laugh. Protect your energy. Experience some form of pleasure every day. Nourish and move your body – not out of hate for it but because you know it boosts your sparkle. Do one small thing towards your life's biggest goal this week, just for fun. No more hiding, no more pretending about who you are, and what you want.

Now is the time to own your life again and embrace your true passions and purpose. Take off the masks you've been wearing to please others. Start living as the woman you were created to be and begin to experience the life you were always meant to have. No apologies or permission needed.

*And there I was…*
*Waiting for the keys.*
*Waiting for that shining knight.*
*That inheritance.*
*That leg up.*
*That hook up.*
*That opening.*
*I greyed, tired and died once or twice while I waited.*
*If only I knew, I was never in chains.*
*Never needed rescuing.*
*Never needed a favour.*
*Could have kicked down any door.*
*Could have remained alive*
*If I'd only realised I carried all I needed inside.*

*Poem by Vean Ima*

My darling sparkle sister, you have all you need inside. Stand up straight, pick up your crown and walk forward as the Queen of your own life. It's time to declare with all your heart, "I'm a woman with sparkle". You've got your sparkle back. You always had it, you just needed to return to it and remember the things that made it shine brightest. Take a deep breath, relax those shoulder because today's the day you step out of the shadows and back into your light. No more waiting, no more hoping, no more not believing in yourself, worth or purpose. Your birth wasn't a mistake, it was a divine command because you and your gifts are needed on the earth at this time. So, go shine like the star that you are because in doing that you'll send a silent command all around the world, letting other women know it's time for them to do the same.

Big love,

*Sally* x

**2 small sparkly actions:**

1) I want you to email me. I'm serious. I want you to put as the email title: 'I'm a woman with sparkle because...' and then I want you to write one sentence about why you're a woman with sparkle. It's important to me (and I believe it's important to put it out in the universe too) that you know at least one small or big reason why you're a woman with sparkle. I may not be able to reply to all the emails directly, but I will read every single one of them because you and your sparkle are super important to me. Email me: mysparkle@womenwithsparkle.com I can't wait to hear about why you're a woman with sparkle.

2) Go to www.womenwithsparkle.com/subscribe and subscribe to my newsletter. You'll then be emailed your **free '7-Day Sparkle Boosting Strategy'** that you can use to super-boost your sparkle this week or whenever you feel a little less than sparkly.

**Want more from me?**

- Twice a year I run my flagship **'Get Your Sparkle Back' course**. It's a 6-week online course with live teaching from me where you'll join other women from around the world who all want more sparkle in their bodies and lives. It's so much fun and if you've enjoyed this book then you'll love this course. Go to www.womenwithsparkle.com/courses to sign up for this or my other courses and masterclasses.

- I work with a handful of private clients to personally help them get to the root cause of any problems they're having and to get their sparkle back. For **1-2-1 coaching** enquiries, please go to www.womenwithsparkle.com and fill out the contact form.

- For all paid **speaking engagements** please email: speaking@womenwithsparkle.com

- Follow me on Instagram for **fun, sparkle and facts** about your fantastic female body @womenwithsparkle

# SPARKLY
# RECOMMENDATIONS

If you want to continue on your sparkle-filled journey, then these are some of the most helpful and empowering resources and products I personally recommend.

## BOOKS TO BOOST YOUR SPARKLE

- **The Woman Code** *Perfect your cycle, amplify your fertility, supercharge your sex drive and become a power source* by Alisa Vitti.

- **Beyond the Pill** *A 30-day program to balance your hormones, reclaim your body, and reverse the dangerous side effects of the birth control pill* by Dr Joelene Brighten.

- **Period Repair Manual** *Natural Treatment for Better Hormones and Better Periods* by Lara Briden.

- **The Wisdom of the Menopause** *Creating physical and emotional health during the change* by Christiane Northrup.

- **Invisible Women** *Exposing data bias in a world designed for men* by Caroline Criado Perez.

- **Fat Doesn't Make You Fat** by Khush Mark (e-book bought from website: www.khushmark.com/services/fat-doesnt-make-you-fat-ebook/)

- **Sweetening The Pill** *or How We Got Hooked on Hormonal Birth Control* by Holly Grigg-Spall.

- **Body Positive Power** *How to stop dieting, make peace with your body and live* by Meghan Jayne Crabbe.

- **Mirror Work** *21 days to heal your life* by Louise Hay.

- **The Beauty Myth** *How images of beauty are used against women* by Naomi Wolf.

- **The End of Overeating** *Taking control of our insatiable appetite* by David A Kessler.

- **The Sleep Revolution** *Transforming your life one night at a time* by Arianna Huffington.

- **The Organised Mum Method** *Transform your home in 30 minutes a day* by Gemma Bray.

## FILMS/DOCUMENTARIES

- Please watch the INCREDIBLE documentary **'Embrace'** with your female family members and friends. <u>bodyimagemovement.com/embrace/see-the-film</u>

- Keep an eye out (it may be released by the time this book has been published) for **'The Business of Birth Control'** <u>www.thebusinessof.life</u>. It's going to be eye-opening and empowering.

## APPS

- **MyFLO Period Tracker** – www.myflotracker.com
  I believe this is an absolute must for all menstruating women.

- **THINKDIRTY** – www.thinkdirtyapp.com – it will show you which of the products you use in your home or on your body have toxic chemicals in that you were likely not aware of.

- **The Team TOMM app**
  www.theorganisedmum.blog/shop-2
  To help you with your housework if it's something that stresses you out.

## ONLINE COURSES

- Various courses are always being created to help boost your sparkle at www.womenwithsparkle.com/courses

## WEBSITES

### Health

These are a treasure trove of articles and help for women's health and hormonal issues (including information on your contraceptive choices). These great women are true pioneers and have helped many struggling women find health and freedom through their work. I'm so grateful for all they do and have taught me.

- **Lara Briden** www.larabriden.com

- **Dr Joelene Brighten** www.drbrighten.com

- **Flo Living** www.floliving.com (by Alisa Vitti)

- **Dr Christiane Northrup** www.drnorthrup.com

- **Khush Mark** www.khushmark.com

## Lifestyle

These women can bring extra calm and sparkle to your life with all they teach and create.

- **Cleaning: The Organised Mum** Gemma Bray has revolutionised my life and reduced my stress so much with housework. She's a total tonic and you can go to her blog www.theorganisedmum.blog , follow her on Instagram @the_organised_mum or download her TeamTOMM app. You need this woman if you get overwhelmed with the day to day jobs of running a household.

- **Calm: Live Three Sixty** www.livethreesixty.com is a website, podcast, and nourishing ecosystem created by the beautiful Tamu Thomas to uplift and inform women, and give them insightful and practical ways to bring more joy to everyday life. I honestly feel calmer just thinking about Tamu, her beautiful voice and bountiful wisdom.

- **Confidence: Louisa Hussey**
  www.louisahussey.com is a transformational EFT practitioner and coach who helps women with their mindset and confidence. She's got buckets of sparkle and can help you with yours.

- **Clothes: Stevie B Styling** www.steviebstyle.com will get you loving your body and dressing so you feel utterly fabulous, whatever your shape or size. She can do everything from overhaul your current wardrobe, give you a whole new look or super-boost your body confidence.

- **Money:** www.you4us.com and www.themoneymedium.com both of these world-changing women can teach you practical ways to manage and improve your money situation and mindset. They're both magical and have helped me so much in this area – which I used to really struggle with.

# PRODUCTS

- **Blue/green light blocking glasses** to help you sleep better. If you have to be on your phone or laptop in the evening www.Safetyblueblockers.com or www.blublox.com

- **The Happy Newspaper**
www.thehappynewspaper.com A newspaper that collates some of the happiest news happening in our world – it's just as important we read this stuff as the negative news that's seen as "normal".

- **Inspirational prints** to have around your home or office to boost your sparkle by Vean Ima prints www.veanimaprints.com and the Unrefined Soul Scribe www.etsy.com/shop/UnrefinedSoul will boost your sparkle with their words and every woman and child should have one of these prints in their home.

- **Clothes and accessories that make you feel fabulous as a woman** www.kemitelford.com These vibrant, bold, and gorgeous clothes are designed by a woman who wants every woman to feel fabulous. Yvonne who owns this brand creates Queens (and the t-shirt I'm wearing on the front of this book is by her). Also www.zoesherwood.co.uk makes 'Empowering and Unifying Adornments' and I think every woman should have one of her 'me' rings.

- **For beautiful sparkly treasures** for you and your children's life www.sparklechild.com – their products are SO beautiful and luxuriously sparkly they'll infuse joy, magic, and, of course, sparkle into your everyday life.

- **My favourite sparkle, health, and beauty-boosting brand** www.glowbarldn.com sell "healing herbs for modern babes" and their adaptogens are great to help reduce stress and balance hormones. If you're in London, you can also visit their incredible café and infrared saunas to super-boost your sparkle.

- **For natural deodorants** – I love Aurelia botanical deodorant (quite pricey but smells heavenly and lasts ages), Norfolk Natural Living natural deodorant in Lime or Dr Organics in Tea Tree. However, with any of these personal or home care products always check them on the ThinkDirty.App as sometimes ingredients get changed.

- **For sanitary products** – for organic disposable pads, liners, and tampons I use Natracare, and for non-disposable pads that are better for the environment and your body, I use the fabulous www.wearemout.co.uk who are a female-run brand literally changing the world with what they're doing.

- **Natural cleaning products** – there are lots of blogs and websites that can show you how to make your own (including The Organised Mum) but if you don't have the time or inclination to make your own then I love the brands Norfolk Natural Living (they also do other gorgeous eco, non-toxic products for your home and skin) www.norfolknaturalliving.com and Kinn www.kinn-living.com

# FOODS/DRINKS

- **For great dairy free milks** without added nasties then I'd recommend the brand 'Plenish' (their cashew nut milk has a creamy taste so perfect for tea/coffee/cereal).

- **For great dairy free cheeses** (although this is all down to your own personal taste) I like to use 'Nush' cream cheese with chives (you'd never know the difference between this and a cow's milk cream cheese) www.nushfoods.co.uk; 'Follow Your Heart' smoked gouda slices www.followyourheart.com or for a dairy free cheese that melts then Applewood Vegan cheese is a winner.

- **For a great dairy free yoghurt** I love www.coyo.com 'Coyo' coconut yoghurt (great for breakfast or to make desserts with in place of cream).

- **For the most divine, dairy-free, pleasure filled chocolate** – www.boojabooja.com Booja booja truffles are just sooo melt in your mouth sexy! My favourites are their honeycomb or hazelnut.

- **Kombucha.** There are lots of great brands and flavours out there and it's all down to personal taste, but I love Hanora Health's Ginger and Lemon kombucha www.hanorahealth.co.uk (I also love their brand and company's ethos), Purely Kombucha www.purelykombucha.co.uk (beautifully made health elixirs), Go Kombucha www.gokombucha.co.uk (their Green Sencha and China White are perfect replacements for white wine/champagne/prosecco) and Kevita's Pineapple Peach and Tart Cherry if you want something that tastes more like a soft drink www.kevita.com

## PERSONAL THANKS

I can't list everyone who's helped me and this book see the light of day – so I thought I wouldn't. I thought I'd just leave it for you to know that if you've ever supported me, been kind to me, helped me through tough times, enjoyed good times with me, laughed with me, cried with me, danced with me, debated with me, encouraged me and accepted me with or without my sparkle, then to you, I'm truly grateful. Thank you to anyone who's believed in me, my passion for helping women to get their sparkle back, and told me to "keep going" when I was struggling with writing this book. I thank you all from the bottom of my sparkly heart.

And even though I don't want to start naming names, because I'd not be able to stop (and I don't like the idea of leaving people out), there are 6 people who I *must* personally thank because without them this book wouldn't be here. Al – for absolutely everything. Charlie – for years of encouraging me. Erica – for heart-centred editing. Jen – for your incredible expertise and coaching. Kish – for your constant health support and love. Ollie - for being a total genius. Without the 6 of you this book wouldn't have been birthed, so thank you.

# PROFESSIONAL ACKNOWLEDGEMENTS

Thank you all for using your gifts to bring this sparkly book to life.

**Editor:** Erica Reed - Profile at www.upwork.com
**Cover photography and artwork:** Ollie Weait
www.ollieweaitphotography.com @ollieweait
**Original cover design:**
Daria Balashova www.dariabalashova.com
**Styling:** Claire Dyer@claire_anne_dyer
**Poem at start of book:**
Nikka Ursula @nikkaursula
**Poem in 'Final Sparkly Sentiment':**
Vean Ima @vean_ima
**Proof readers:**
Mgnlondon.com, Charlie Baker, Ariane Signer,
Carly Moosah, Helen Hanson

Printed in Great Britain
by Amazon